Souls
in
Prison

SOULS IN PRISON

Manford George Gutzke

THOMAS NELSON INC., PUBLISHERS
Nashville / New York

Library of Congress Cataloging in Publication Data:

Gutzke, Manford George.
  Souls in Prison.

  1. Christian life—1960–   I. Title.
B 501.2.G87   248'.4   74–32468

ISBN 0–8407–5587–2

Contents

THE JUDGMENT OF GOD

IN CAPTIVITY

YET THERE IS HOPE

*Souls
in
Prison*

The Law
of God

Have you ever wondered about the beginning of God? "Before the mountains were brought forth, or ever thou hadst formed the earth and the world, even from everlasting to everlasting, thou art God." These are the words of the Psalmist, in the 90th Psalm, in the 2nd verse. And this is the expression of the confidence of all people who believe in God.

God Is Eternal

All spiritual experience comes from man's thinking about God. If a man feels and thinks that God is and that God is aware of him and that God cares for him, then a man's heart and mind can be affected by his thoughts of God.

You see, whenever you find a person who really believes in the God and Father of our Lord Jesus Christ, the heart of that Christian is a reconciled heart. And there is a loving fellowship with God as Father; because the Christian, deep down in his own soul, has the mind and the will of Jesus Christ, who looks upon the Father with love and devotion. For this reason the Christian finds himself saying from his heart, "Abba, Father." As he looks to God, he experiences something that I want to talk about. He knows God is eternal. The Christian can say from the bottom of his heart in the words of that great 90th Psalm, "Lord, thou hast been our dwelling place in all generations."

And so we say God is eternal. Now the word "eternal" is a strange word. You and I would seldom use it. It's difficult to grasp. Simply put, we can say it means something that's unending, everlasting, always is and was and will be. No beginning, no ending. And right away someone will say, "Well, that's impossible. There's no such thing as something without a beginning or ending." By the way, while you're wondering about that, if I had a straight line, you'd say it has a beginning and an ending. But what about a circle? Where does it start? Where does it stop? You see, the fact that you speak of a thing as having no beginning and no ending does not necessarily mean it can't exist. Eternity is inconceivable to our minds; and yet it means always. And by the way, when you say that God is eternal, you mean He had no yesterday and will have no tomorrow. When you're speaking of the Eternal God, you're thinking about One who does not see anything as yesterday and does not see anything as tomorrow. He sees it all at the same time.

With God, Calvary did not happen 1900 years ago. Calvary is now. You could speak of the Eternal God as being in "the everlasting now"; that it is always present with God. Calvary, with everything that happened on it, is to be seen in God's eyes now. Not only does He see the end from the beginning, but also right now He knows how it's going to be with us, and right now He knows where we're going to be.

You'll remember that in the Book of Hebrews, the 13th chapter and the 8th verse, we have a line that speaks of "Jesus Christ the same yesterday, and today, and for ever." This has a profound effect on the heart and mind of any human being, because with us there are so many changes. Things are being made different all the time. In one of the familiar hymns you will remember you have these lines: "Change and decay in all around I see. Oh, thou who changest not, abide with me." I like that! "Change and decay"—things becoming different, and things going to ruin. "In all around I see"—that's the way it is in this world. "Oh, thou who changest not"—no deterioration and no ruin. "Abide with me"—come to me and keep me from changing.

Now this idea that God is eternal is in the heart of every Christian, and this is the basis of the Christian's rest. Any person who really and truly believes in God should have in mind that His Word is forever. "Forever O Lord, thy Word is settled in Heaven." It's an eternal Word. You read, "Whosoever believeth in Me shall not perish but have everlasting life"—it's forever, always true! "Come unto Me and I will give you rest"—it's forever, always true! "I will never leave thee nor forsake thee"—forever, always true! You can have that promise at all times. And this is the ground of the peace of heart and mind that comes to a believer—"the peace of God that passeth all understanding." No one else could understand it, but you do. It rests in the Word of God, and is anchored in the very Being of God; it is forever. The Christian has an assurance God is not going to change.

If you look out at a mountain, you think it's been there forever, but that mountain once upon a time was raised to that height and sometime will come down from that height. God will never change. You can put your whole trust, your whole confidence in the Living God. There He is! He will always be that way! There'll never be variableness in Him. He'll be steadfast all the way. In the world there is much that's changing. Like the waves of the sea, the things of the world toss and roll, and they run and toss, all the time. But even though you're sailing on the ocean and the waves are running by you in any direction the wind happens to blow, the sailor has a compass, and the compass is steady. The compass points to the north, no matter if the wind's blowing from the west or from the south or from the east—or there's no wind at all. The compass is steady. If I put my trust in God and believe in the Lord Jesus Christ and walk with Him, I can expect that in me something will become settled—permanent. I won't ever have to change. God will always be there.

Now some people have the feeling that the Bible speaks about God repenting in the sense that He changed His mind. He told Jonah to go and preach to Nineveh that in forty days Nineveh would be destroyed, and then it didn't happen that way. But if you look into that, you'll find that God said to Jonah, *"They* changed *their* ways, and so I changed what I was going to do." But I have been helped by that when I think about this: Can you picture yourself riding in a bus, down the road? Let us say that you've come up to a schoolhouse. As you're coming along the road, the schoolhouse is in front of you. The bus moves along. After awhile the schoolhouse is beside you. Then the schoolhouse is behind you. Well now, in your traveling on that day, first you had the schoolhouse in front of you, then beside you, then behind you. Did that mean that the schoolhouse moved? The schoolhouse didn't move. What happened? You moved! So it is with God.

God is an eternal Being, unchangeable, everlasting in Himself. Now all of this eternal character of God comes to us in the Person of Jesus Christ. And in Christ Jesus who in one place in the Bible is spoken of as The Everlasting Father, the eternal reality of God comes into our souls.

Do you know what being holy really means? In Leviticus 11:44 and 45 we read, "For I am the Lord your God: ye shall therefore sanctify yourselves, and ye shall be holy; for I am holy: neither shall ye defile yourselves with any manner of creeping thing that creepeth upon the earth. For I am the Lord that bringeth you up out of the land of Egypt, to be your God: ye shall therefore be holy, for I am holy." Peter quotes this in the New Testament saying, "As it is written, be ye holy, for I am holy."

God Is Holy

The Christian Gospel tells the world how a man can be in fellowship with a holy God, and how we can deal with God, and how God is revealed to the heart—to the consciousness of man. A Christian is nothing in himself, by his own strength. If a Christian can stand the way we commonly expect him to, and be faithful in all circumstances, and no matter what the situation is, be consistent, that's because he's standing on the Rock of Ages. A man can't stand if he is in sinking sand. A man can't stand if he is in soft mud. You have to have something to stand on, and a Christian stands on something. He stands on the Rock of Ages. He stands on the reality of God.

At a certain stage in Israel's national affairs, the people of Israel actually lost the liberty they had in God. They lost the freedom that they had been given in God. They lost the blessing that they had been given in God. A person who believes in the Lord can actually lose his liberty and his freedom and his blessing because of the way in which he acts. I realize that some who read this have never really come to a definite relationship with God through Jesus Christ. I hope you will be patient. You think it all through just as critically as you want to. I'll try and make it clear to you what the Bible teaches about this whole matter. Just now we're concerned about being a real Christian.

In order to understand what really happened when the believers in the time of Israel lost their freedom, we'll have to see who these people really were. They were not the people of God because they were exceptional people. They were not the people of God because they were stronger, or better, or wiser, or more of them than anybody else. As a matter of fact, there were not more of them than anyone else, and actually their history shows that they weren't any stronger, that they weren't any better, they really weren't any wiser. You will ask, then what made them the people of God? They were the people of God because when God called them, they came and committed themselves to Him. But they were the same kind of people you would find anywhere in the world.

You see, we need to understand that when a person becomes a Christian, he doesn't become an angel. Just because you believe in the Lord Jesus Christ isn't going to make you perfect. Now, we're criticized for that by the people of the world. When a man or woman becomes a Christian, right in his own family, right in his own home, he's going to have to endure criticism and sometimes sneering sarcasm from people who say, "Well now, I thought because you were a Christian you were going to be perfect. I thought we'd never have any more trouble with you.

Well, if the Christian who led you to the Lord was wise, he did not say you were going to be perfect, and he did not say you would never make a mistake again. That's not the object! It's just like a person going to the hospital. Just because a man goes to the hospital and comes out cured does not mean he never will be sick again. As a matter of fact, he went to the hospital because he was prone to sickness. So it is with reference to Christians. We do not come to God because we're good. Christians aren't people who are better than anyone else. Christians are people who come to God in need. They need help, and they understand that in the Gospel of the Lord Jesus Christ this help is offered to them. They belong to Him, and they commit themselves to God.

The outstanding thing about a Christian person is that he is depending on God. I want to emphasize it is God who makes the difference. God makes the difference in the world outside, and He makes the difference in the Christian himself in his own personal experience. Whatever may be your personal experience, remember this: it's the reality of God that will make the difference in your soul.

It is important, though, to point out that this God in whom we trust is holy. Do you know what being holy really means? Well the word "holy" is related to the English word "wholly." When you speak of holiness, you're talking about the whole thing. When you speak about the whole thing, you mean one hundred percent of it. When everything is done from a one hundred percent point of view, then it's wholly the one thing. When you say God is holy, you mean He's one hundred percent whatever He is—and what He is is all good. When you say "God is holy," you mean He's absolutely honest, fair and square.

A common expression we used when I was a boy was that a person is "all wool and a yard wide." That was referring to woolen cloth, when there was no mixture and everything was genuine, and full measured. Another way of speaking about God being holy is to say that when He is dealing with you, He'll "give you sixteen ounces to the pound." He is one hundred percent. He is absolutely whatever He sets out to be.

God is benevolent. He's going to be kind to you; He's going to be helpful—one hundred percent. No reservation. You say you're not much? He's still benevolent. You're not faithful? He's still benevolent. God is benevolent—one hundred percent. That is to say, He is holy. God is good. There is no limit to His goodness—it endureth forever. On and on and on and on, God will be good. Your own life and experiences are spotty. Sometimes you have good days, sometimes bad days. Don't blame that on God. God is good all the time. He's good in the sunshine; He's good in the rain. He's good when it's cold, He's good when it's hot. With His goodness, there is no limit. God is faithful. There is no faltering; you can depend on Him. When you say God is merciful, you mean He is merciful all the way!

In Psalm 145:17 you read "The Lord is righteous in all his ways, and holy in all his works." Whenever you think of the holiness of God, think of something that is one hundred percent—three feet to the yard, sixteen ounces to the pound, and everything He's supposed to be. Anything He is, He is altogether. If He's going to take care of you, He'll take care of you one hundred percent. He'll watch over you at all times, "The Keeper of Israel neither slumbers nor sleeps."

Do you think rules are any help in living? "Wherefore the law was our schoolmaster to bring us unto Christ, that we might be justified by faith." This is the way the Apostle Paul comments on the significance of the law in the life of a believer. The law does have a function. The question often comes up, whether or not a believer in Christ should know the Ten Commandments and be acquainted with the law. I think Paul would say, "Yes indeed!" because the Christian starts out as just an ordinary human being. And the ordinary human being needs to be taught what in the sight of God is right and what is wrong. This will be shown to him in the Ten Commandments and the law. And so the law is "a schoolmaster" showing us right and wrong, to bring us to Christ, that we might be justified by faith. The law of God makes us realize ourselves to be wrong and know that the only way for us to be accepted with God is to accept Jesus Christ. By believing in Him, we find that we actually are justified.

The Ten Words

Our interest in this chapter is in the life and experience of Christians. We're studying about believers, and we're particularly interested in believers at a certain stage in their experience. When we look into the history of Israel, we will see Israel at a point where God's people were actually robbed of their benefits. They were robbed of their liberty and prevented from having their freedom and the things they had gained by being in the will of God. We raise the question of how this can be.

We find that it's possible for believers who belong to God and are in the relationship with God to actually be made prisoners because of sin.

In order for us to fully understand this, we must study the nature of a Christian. What does it actually mean to be a Christian? Well, one thing about a Christian is that he has the law of God in the Ten Words. When people believe in God, they believe in Someone who is eternal, and they believe in Someone who is holy. They are conscious that the Eternal God is their refuge and that the Holy God is their Savior. These people also have been instructed in the law of God. The children of Israel had the law of God and had been instructed in it.

Now what does this mean? What is the law of God? What did they have when they had His law? If you have the law of God, it's basic to remember that God *is*. And He is unchangeable forever. He is always the same. Now the *way* God is, we call His law. If a man wants to have something to do with God, what will the ways of God require of him? Well, that was set forth in what the Bible calls the Ten Words. If you look at the original writings, you will see that when the children of Israel gathered together and Moses went up the Mount and received the Table of Stone, upon them were engraved "the Ten Words." Now the Ten Words, or the Ten Commandments as we commonly call them, set the pattern of righteousness that is acceptable to God.

Look at that pattern of righteousness and you will see right away how broad and comprehensive it is and how it covers the whole range of human activity. Human beings generally deal with at least three classes of people. First there is the class that is over them, to whom they are responsible. And that goes all the way up to the very Person of God. Toward those people who are over them, Christians will show reverence—especially toward God. Secondly there are those people who are equal to you. They are the same kind of folks you are, and you will have consideration for them. Thirdly there are people in the world who are not as fortunate as you. They are in need compared to you, and toward those people the right thing to do is have charity.

Now I have mentioned these three lines along which a person will act if he's right in God's sight. Toward God, he will show reverence. You'll find that in the first four commandments. "Thou shalt have no other gods before me." Above everything else, "Thou shalt worship the Lord thy God, and Him only shalt thou serve." Then again, "Thou shalt not make any graven images of God." Don't think for one moment that you can make a man-size image of God. And you must respect His Name—do not "take the name of the Lord thy God in vain." That does not only refer to profanity. It means don't go through the motions of public prayer if you don't mean it. Don't go through the motions of public worship if you don't mean it. If you're coming into the presence of God, be genuine and sincere. And if you're not that, you're actually "taking the name of the Lord thy God in vain." And the last thing would be to respect the Sabbath Day and keep it holy. These rules indicate what right living will be in the sight of God with reference to Himself, in reverence.

Next is respect toward those who are your equals, or

who are over you. You will remember in the fifth com-
mandment we are told, "Thou shalt honor thy father
and thy mother." Honoring your father and mother,
honoring the persons who have control over you and
who have responsibility for you, is a right thing in the
sight of God. And then there are all the other commandments: "Thou shalt not kill; Thou shalt not steal;
Thou shalt not bear false witness." Have consideration
for those who are your equals and charity toward the
poor.

I have quickly sketched here the pattern of conduct
that is reflected in the Ten Commandments—acts and
attitudes that are right in the sight of God. By the way,
there's only One Person who ever lived on earth that
kept those laws perfectly, and that was Jesus of Nazareth. He obeyed the law in every point. But the Christian
has the law as a measure for what is to be expected of
him. The law has the same value to a Christian that a
warning fence has along a highway in a mountain road.
You may have a row of whitewashed posts with chains
from one to the other to warn you of the edge of the
precipice. Or you might just have guidelines painted on
the pavement itself to warn you. Now that warning
paint will never make your car run. It won't actually
push the car along, but it will guide you, and that's the
way it is with the law. It's like rails to a railroad train. The
rails have no power to push the train, but they can guide
the train when it operates, and that's the way it is with
the law. The law guides any person who wants to do the
right thing in the sight of God.

And by the way, the law that the Christian has includes not only the requirements in the Ten Words, but also the tabernacle and the sacrifices that the worshiper can follow to be forgiven his sins and be made properly fit for the presence of God. All of these things are set forth in the law, and the believer has it as his guide. The believer has a great many actual useful elements in him. He has faith in the eternal God; he is in contact with the Holy God; he has a knowledge of the requirements of God in the Ten Words—the Ten Commandments.

Do you think sin ever changes? The testimony of the Bible is that "the wages of sin is death." I'm satisfied that a good many people will read this book who have never come to a definite relationship with God through the Lord Jesus Christ. Will you do so now? Those of us who know the Christian Gospel are happy to tell the whole wide world that the sinner can be forgiven. You can be reconciled to God. We have been, and

The Wages of Sin

we know it is true. A Christian is a person who has been reconciled to God by the work of Jesus Christ. In that sense, the Christian has dealt with the problem of sin which confronts every human. But we're going to see that the Christian stands in danger of losing his benefits. A Christian can lose his liberty—he can lose, as it were, his freedom. I want to tell you how this can happen, but I also want you to know that the man we're talking about is a real Christian. Later we'll discuss the wages of sin, and we have seen that "the wages of sin is death." We can say that the Christian when he was reconciled to God dealt at the very outset with the problem of sin. But we need to see that sin is not done with the Christian. Sin sticks to him, and as long as he lives in this world, he's going to have it to deal with. Fortunately he can have victory over it, but he'll always have it to deal with.

Sin is a "God word." Sin is to God what darkness is to light. The only way you can understand what darkness is, is to know what light is, for darkness is the absence of light. If you know what life is, you can figure out what death is, because death is just the absence of life. If you know who God is, you can figure out what sin is because anything unlike God is sin.

Every now and again we get the impression that people in our day have lost their aversion to sin. Sin is not as bad as it used to be in people's minds. What that actually is saying is that the concept of God has been reduced. If you have a small God, you'll have a small idea of sin. If you have a great God, then sin will be a serious thing. Sin is a word that belongs to God. If you have no idea of God, you certainly won't have any idea of sin. Sin is the way you refer to a person's conduct that is not like God.

In Christ Jesus, this disposition of sinning, this actual experience of sinning, can be forgiven. That isn't a provision made for just a few people. Actually the Bible teaches us there is no man who is sinless. "All have sinned and come short of the glory of God." "There is none righteous, no not one." But in Christ there is forgiveness, and not only is there forgiveness from the guilt and the penalty of sin, but also there is deliverance from its power. This is something people need to know more about. It's easy to be foolish. Even after some people know Jesus Christ as their Savior, know that their sins are forgiven, they go out and do foolish things. They fall into sin. People can be foolish even after they have found out there is salvation in the Lord. When we say "a Christian falls into sin," we don't mean that he's consciously doing wrong. Sin can be a condition or a frame of mind. It can be a wrong standing before God. You can be in the state of sin. You can have sin in your body in such a way that when a situation comes up you act sinfully. Then the condition becomes an act you actually perform. You can perform three sins before breakfast and ten sins between breakfast and lunch—acts of sin you can count. Believers can fall into sin even though they're forgiven already. It's a good deal like having weeds in a garden. One of the tragedies of farming is that when you plant beans in the garden it is as though during the night an enemy comes and sows other seeds there. You will grow things in that garden that you didn't plant. You may plant only beans, but you will have weeds too. In fact, a garden can be so overrun with weeds that you don't get any beans at all. And you can actually have sin getting such deep root that you are in grave danger of being shut away from God. You can be overcome by weeds.

Now the form of sin may change, just like fashion. The style of hats changes, and the style of dresses—and also the style of sin. But it will always have the same element. Sin is a form of self-indulgence and self-pleasing. Think of self-interest as an appetite—the things that your body would like to have. Think of self-satisfaction as imagination—the things that are pleasing to you. So then self, in its appetite and its imagination and in its vanity, can generate sin. Those of you who are believers in the Lord Jesus Christ will possibly say "Well I'm against sin. I don't want anything to do with it." I'd like to say to you very gently, sin may stick with you anyway. You may have it all round about you. It's important for you to realize that sin is a very common condition. Remember, though, that sin can be forgiven. It can be set aside. Yet as far as the Christian is concerned, that sin is around him and clings to him and makes it necessary for him to act very definitely to acknowledge it, to recognize it. The most important thing is the recognition that you could fall into it. It is like realizing that if you are going to have a garden, you not only need to get the land plowed, and buy the beans you are going to plant, but you must be prepared to be there with a hoe and dig out the weeds. Because sin will persist.

Perhaps you would say to me, "But Christ Jesus will save me from it." That's true! "And the blood of Jesus Christ will cleanse us from all sin." That's true! But I also want to tell you that the presence of sin, unless you confess it, unless you put your finger on it, unless you repudiate it, will actually disqualify you from blessings to be received. You can actually become barren and fruitless because of sin.

"Thy word have I hid in mine heart, that I might not sin against thee" (Psalm 119:11). And then there is the warning, "Let not sin therefore reign in your mortal body, that ye should obey it in the lusts thereof. Neither yield ye your members as instruments of unrighteousness unto sin: but yield yourselves unto God, as those that are alive from the dead, and your members as instruments of righteousness unto God." This is the way Paul puts it in Romans 6:12-13.

When the children of Israel were being called out of Egypt to walk with God, and God revealed to them through Moses His law, they had requirements for pleasing God. But even after that, those people fell into sin, time and time again. And it was always true that when sin came, judgment would need to come, and the people would need to get right with God. It's still that way with us today.

Do you realize sin can be forgiven? "If we confess our sins, he is faithful and just to forgive us our sins, and to cleanse us from all unrighteousness." In the last chapter we talked about sin. I expect not many Christians felt inspired while they were thinking about it. I hope that I was able to keep before your mind that the thing to do with sin is confess it. But now I have something quite a bit brighter to bring to your attention.

The Forgiveness of Sins

Sin is here—around us and in us. There isn't any question that it can harm us—do us real injury. There's no doubt about the human tendency to sin. But here is the greatest thing I can ever say to you about sin: it can be forgiven.

You may not be ready to think about that right now. Maybe you're wondering if you'll get enough money to pay your bills, whether you'll get your work done today, whether you can hold onto your job, whether you have to put up with your neighbor, whether you'll be able to sell your house. You may be thinking about all kinds of things. But it's possible that at one time or another as a Christian, you wonder about the things you've done wrong. After all, it isn't the bad people in the world who are bothered about sin; it's the good people. It's the people who don't want to do wrong and feel badly when they have done wrong. I want to tell you that sin can be forgiven. The blood of Christ can cleanse us from all sin. There is nothing a human being can do that God cannot forgive in Christ Jesus. It's impossible for a human being to commit any kind of sin that Christ Jesus cannot completely and fully forgive and cleanse.

It would be a wonderful thing to find out you could accept Jesus Christ and from that time on, you'd never do anything wrong. But that's not the truth. The truth of the matter is that even after they know the Lord Jesus Christ people can fall into ways of doing things that are displeasing to God. But the wonderful thing is, this can be forgiven. But I need to stress to you that sin must be confessed. "He that covereth his sins shall not prosper." Man does not want to admit that he has done wrong. No matter how wrong he's been, he wants to have some way of explaining it, or claim it isn't as bad as it looks. Pride causes man to alibi. And this is very foolish, because God sees through us, absolutely and altogether. He knows all about us.

Now there is a dangerous error I should mention in passing. Somehow or other the idea has gotten out that because Christ Jesus died for man, then everybody has been forgiven. Actually all *can* be forgiven. "Whosoever will" can come to Him, and he will be forgiven. I know that from personal experience! Anyone who confesses and repents will be forgiven by Jesus Christ. But if a person doesn't come to the Lord and doesn't confess, then he *won't* be forgiven, and we need to remember that too. Sin must be confessed in order that we may benefit by the work of Christ Jesus that was done for us.

Among those reading these words there will be any number who have no personal relation with God. God may be watching over you. He may be acting as an umpire, but you don't feel like admitting to God that you have done anything wrong in His sight. There is just one message for you. You must accept Christ Jesus as your Savior from sin. You must first receive the grace of God in Jesus Christ, and then more can happen to you.

Maybe you are already a believer. You understand that Christ Jesus is the Savior, that He came into the world to seek and to save the lost, that He gave His life a ransom for many. You are among those who believed this, and you accepted Him because you really and truly believed in Him. Yet you may have done wrong. You may have fallen into sin. As a believer you must confess. The unsaved person must accept Christ and plead guilty for all parts of his life. The Lord God will forgive him and cleanse him. But the believer, who on a given day may do wrong, must confess. He must come into the presence of God and confess the thing that was wrong.

I am not too concerned that he confess to a man. Sometimes it helps to confess to another human being because it gets your words out. But that's not essential. The other human being can't forgive you. Only God can forgive your sins, and God *will* forgive you when you come to Him. I remember years ago when I first became a Christian. I was in the Canadian Army in the first World War. I had gone into very few churches where the Gospel was preached. But I went to a church in Hamilton, Ontario, and there I heard the Gospel preached—and as the preacher was ministering the Gospel, to my great surprise, he said if there was anybody present who needed help he could come down and talk to him. I was just a young soldier at the time, and I decided to go down and ask him a question. So I went down to the front, which I had never done before in my life, and I talked with one of the elders there, and I asked him this question: "Suppose a person has believed in the Lord Jesus Christ but now he realizes that there is something he has done that is wrong. Now what does he do?" And so this kindly man looked at me and said, "Have you forgotten the story of the Prodigal? What was there for the Prodigal to do? All the Prodigal had to do was to come home and confess. He just came to his father and said, 'Father, I have sinned and am not worthy to be called thy son. Make me as one of thy hired servants.'" And so this good man showed me that the thing to do was to confess my sin.

Psalm 51 is a Psalm of confession by a person who believes in God but he hasn't done right, and so he confesses it that way. In the New Testament this is very much like the word "repent"—which does not mean being sorry for it. There is such a thing as being sorry for sin, but that's a good deal like crying over spilt milk. Someone may say, "Oh, I know what you mean. You mean that repentance is a promise to do better." But you don't keep your promises, and God's not likely to be impressed by your pledge to do better. No, I'll tell you what repentance is: a judgment upon self. I judge myself to be unworthy. Paul encourages us by saying, "If we would judge ourselves, we should not be judged." And so what the Bible teaches us at this point about the forgiveness of sins is that the believer should acknowledge his sin, should confess his sin, and should look to the Lord God about it and believe in the forgiveness that has been provided for him.

Probably someone will ask, "Won't repeated confession foster sinning?" It's something to think about. If a man confesses that he sinned, he's forgiven. And he confesses again that he sinned, and he's forgiven. And he confesses again that he has sinned, and he's forgiven again. Will that not foster sin? No, I can tell from personal experience it's not going to foster sinning. Because if you come into the presence of the Lord honestly and sincerely, and name the very sin you did by the name that the Bible gives it, and just acknowledge to the Lord this is the way in which you've lived, and confess it before Him, that won't encourage you to sin more. It will incline us to repent. We cannot avoid sin, but thank God, we can confess it and be forgiven.

The
People
Of God

In comparing men who want the blessing of God, would you have any idea what was so different about Abraham? "Wherefore come out from among them, and be ye separate, saith the Lord, and touch not the unclean thing; and I will receive you, and will be a Father unto you, and ye shall be my sons and daughters, saith the Lord Almighty." These words are quoted by Paul in 2 Corinthians 6:17-18. They give you a clue as to

The Covenant with Abraham

what characterizes the people of God. We'll be noticing in the history of God's people a time when they were not being blessed. This is in a way remarkable because if they were the people of God you would expect them to be blessed. And yet there came a time in their history when they were not blessed. They worked hard, but they had no results; they went through the exercises of praying, but they had no power; they went out to sow in the field, but they had no crop. They were trying to trust God, but they had no peace. This is the condition we are going to be thinking about as we study the nation of Israel in their captivity. They lost their liberty because they were taken as prisoners of war, and they lost their power. So let us ask the question, "Who are these people of God?"

One of the things that is said about them is that thay are the children of Abraham. That's why I asked you what was so different about Abraham. And what does it mean to say that the people of God today are the children of Abraham? The Bible tells us that this means they walk as

Abraham walked. So once again we raise the question: what then made Abraham so unique? It's a very simple but profound thing—he was obedient. He was called to go into a land where he had never been before, and he went out by faith, although he didn't know where he was going. "He went out not knowing whither he went." So initially, the whole experience of Abraham as a child of God and as a man of God, blessed of God, started when God called him and Abraham obeyed. The source of all the blessing of Abraham was in the grace of God, and those who walk in the footsteps of Abraham are also those who share and receive the grace of God.

We say that Abraham received the blessing of God by faith, but that means obedience to the will of God. Abraham obeyed God, and God blessed him. In the course of the history of Abraham, several ideas stand out very clearly. "Now the Lord had said unto Abram, Get thee out of thy country." That was the first thing. A person's country is his natural origin—where he was born. That takes in your father, your mother, your grandparents, your uncles and aunts and all your folk, and it takes in the community that you live in. It takes in your culture. So here you have a believing person and you say to him, "Get out from your natural self, your natural origin, the heredity that you have inherited, everything that you've gotten from your folks, and the social culture that you've shared in the community where you are." Getting out from it means that you don't put your trust in it. It's surprising how many of us plan to be just like our forebears. What they feared, we fear; what they trusted, we trust; what they earned, we

have. The call from God is, "Get out from it." You're not
to depend upon the country in which you grew up or the
family from which you came. I want you to notice the
very essence of obedience is a willingness to let go of
yourself and let God have His way. It is a willingness to
turn away from every advantage that you have because
you were born where you were. It doesn't necessarily
mean these things are bad. It just means you need to be
free to obey. You need to be free to go, so you get out in
order that you may be free. Then God says, "I will make
of thee a great nation." You don't have to build it or
work it up for yourself. God says He will give you a
standing in the community and will increase your sta-
ture in the minds of men. "I will bless thee, I will make
thy name great, and thou shalt be a blessing."

Now this is what God is going to do for those who
obey Him—something Abraham didn't have to work
for. And then follows this further word, "I will bless
them that bless thee, and curse him that curseth thee:
and in thee shall all families of the earth be blessed."
You see, although God is calling Abraham out from
people, it isn't to separate him from people. It's just to
get him out there where God can deal with him and use
him. So He's saying to Abraham, "If you're going to get
from Me a pail full of honey, the first thing you have to
do is empty the water out." This is an idea that can be
very easily put into words, but not so easily put into
action. Would you like to have the blessing of God in
your life? Then you'll need to be willing to let go of
yourself and everything you have, and turn yourself
over to God—today! The people of God will be marked

by their willingness to be separate. But they will also be marked by blessing. The astounding fact is that people who are sold out to God will be blessed, and they will be taken care of. And they will also be marked by distinction. Their experience will be unique.

What will be different about the experience of God's people? Well for one thing, with chaos all around them, God's people can be quiet. They will have quietness in the midst of chaos. With turmoil everywhere, God's people can be at peace. That doesn't mean they're not involved in life. It means they're convinced that nothing is going to happen that God isn't in control of. You may think people like that are losing out so far as this world is concerned; but you watch them, and you'll find that they have power.

But I want you to think about these people for a moment—people who have been separated from the world in obedience to God. Would it be possible for them ever to lose their blessing? Well, as a matter of fact, in the Old Testament they did, and we're going to try to find out why. We're going to look into that part of the history of the children of Israel when their land was defeated and destroyed, when the people were captured and led away as prisoners by their enemies. And so there were souls in prison among believing people.

Do you know how a sinner could change his record before God? "For on that day shall the priest make an atonement for you, to cleanse you, that ye may be clean from all your sins before the Lord" (Leviticus 16:30). In trying to understand the people of God, it is important to know how the Bible presents them in their character and in their history. You see, when talking about the people of God, we don't mean what the

The Atonement Through Sacrifice

public means by it. We're not picking this word up from the street; we're not taking it out of the newspaper. We're taking the phrase, "the people of God" out of the Bible.

There are some people, of course, who are inclined to think that everybody belongs to God. Well, it's true that He made all men. When you're speaking of "the people of God," however, you don't mean the creatures of God. Anybody whose heart is beating would have to acknowledge that God gives him the strength of that heartbeat. More than that, God is sovereign. The events that take place on the face of the earth, no matter how haphazard they may seem, are under His control. He is also the Judge of all men. And this Almighty God, the Creator, dealing with mankind all over the world, insists that so far as men are concerned, "all have sinned and come short of the glory of God." In another Scripture verse He says "There is none righteous, no not one." So taking the natural man as he is, you wouldn't have anybody naturally qualified to belong to what we would call "the people of God."

The people we speak of as "the people of God," then, are still just human beings. They're not God's people because they're good or virtuous. The truth of the matter is, so far as mankind is concerned, man is doomed because of sin. But "God so loved the world, that he gave his only begotten Son, that whosoever believeth in him should not perish, but have everlasting life." The Bible tells us that God provided salvation for men, and since man was bankrupt he couldn't possibly have bought and paid for it. So when God provided this salvation, he made it free. It had to be free because man didn't have anything to give.

"But when the fullness of the time was come, God sent forth His Son, made of a woman, made under the law, to redeem them that were under the law" (Galatians 4:4-5). But even before Christ came, "in the fullness of time," there was a promise that had been given. And that was the promise that had been given to Abraham, that all that man needs, everything Abraham needed, was given to him freely without cost. Right now, let's consider one aspect of that need. What man really needs most before God is that his sin should be removed. He has his guilt and the responsibility for sin, and then he has his actual involvement in sin. His own disposition is actually affected by this contrary purpose to please himself. He needs to be delivered from sin— from its guilt and its power.

This was pictured in Old Testament times by something that was spoken of as the "atonement." I know that this word does not ordinarily come up in everyday language, but I'm hoping you will know it. The noun "atonement" comes, of course, from the verb "atone"—and that is one verb that has no Latin or Greek root. If you look at it, you'll see the word can be broken into two small words: *at one*. And that's what it really means—*at one-ment*. It has in it the idea of being reconciled, when two parts are brought together as one, when the broken parts are reunited. You see the great truth is that sin separated man from God. And because sin separated and alienated man away from God, there must be the removal of sin, if the man is to be blessed and made a member of the people of God.

You'll remember that the removal of sin is pictured in the Old Testament by blood sacrifice. The altar was the place of sacrifice, and to the altar the worshipper came. A marvelous truth is set forth here. There can be a substitution, indeed there has been inasmuch as Christ has taken my sins and yours upon Himself on the cross. This is what we mean when we speak of believers being purchased by the blood of the Lord Jesus Christ. We would have been alienated from God if Christ Jesus hadn't died for us and paid the price in His own blood. Now we say according to Bible language that "We're not our own, we've been bought with a price." This is true for all the people of God, so if you are one who believes in the Lord Jesus Christ it's true about you. In Christ Jesus you're forgiven your sins, the guilt is taken away, and you are reconciled to God. You are actually made "at one."

We believing people, all who actually put our trust in

the Lord Jesus Christ, receive from God His blessing. We are considered the people of God in a very special way. We are the redeemed ones—the ones who've been bought and paid for, actually privileged to have fellowship with God, even though we were sinners and had done wrong. We can now have fellowship with God because no longer is there any charge against us. There is no debt we need to pay. No charge remains against the believer because all the charges have been paid for by his Lord and Savior, Jesus Christ. This is the fulfillment of the verse with which the chapter began: "On that day shall the priest make an atonement for you, to cleanse you, that ye may be clean from all your sins before the Lord."This is true of the believer. He has believed in the Lord Jesus Christ and the blood of the Lord Jesus Christ will cleanse him from all sin. When God looks on him He sees one for whom Christ died. And as such, the believer is allowed to go free.

Perhaps we should ask ourselves the question: isn't it strange to think that people like this should ever wander away from God? Isn't it strange to think that a person reconciled to God, atoned for by the death of the Lord Jesus Christ, would wander away? But some can and do wander away, and we need to keep them in mind when we think about the captivity of the people of God in the time of Israel. Because we're going to see that these people for whom atonement had been made could actually fall into a snare and be alienated from God.

Have you any idea what advantages a man has when he belongs to the people of God? "Wherefore say unto the children of Israel, I am the Lord, and I will bring you out from under the burdens of the Egyptians, and I will rid you out of their bondage, and I will redeem you with a stretched out arm, and with great judgments: and I will take you to me for a people, and I will be to you a God: and ye shall know that I am the Lord your God, which bringeth you out from under the burdens of the Egyptians. And I will bring you in unto the land, concerning the which I did swear to give it to Abraham, to Isaac, and to Jacob; and I will give it you for an heritage: I am the Lord" (Exodus 6:6-8).

The Guidance of God

In these positive words the promise was made to Moses, to convey to the children of Israel what God would do. We often wish today, I am sure, that we could have such definite assurance of what God will do for us. Well, I would like to tell you that we do have this assurance in the Gospel of the Lord Jesus Christ. I wish everybody on earth knew what is available in Christ Jesus. We have to express it in the language that we use in speaking. When we talk to you about things that pertain to men, we use human words. Then we talk to you about things that pertain to God as we find them in the Bible, and we use Scriptural words. When we're expounding to you what the Bible teaches, we travel through the Scriptures using Old and New Testament. We use the Old Testament because Almighty God inspired the ancient writers to set forth certain truths that are helpful to us. "This truth was written aforetime for our learning that we through patience and comfort of the Scriptures might have hope."

I hope you can feel the promise this chapter opens with the way it would come to us today. You see, everything we have in the Christian Gospel is free, and freely offered to "whosoever will" receive it. I want you to see one of the great benefits that the people of God have. Because of our human limitations and handicaps, life is a very complicated thing. Living is a good deal like taking a journey through a strange country; surroundings are unfamiliar and the footing underneath is treacherous. We've never been on this road before. Every task we pick up to perform, we never did that one before. Every aspect of life that we live, we never did that before. That's true for natural living, but it's just as true for a Christian. You'll know what I mean when I say every day is a new experience—you haven't been through that one before. But here is the great blessing for the people of God—God will watch over you and guide you. The providence of God, of course, extends to all men alike. The sun shines and the rain falls on the good and the bad alike. But there is something special for the people of God, for He is able to make all things work for good to those who love Him. So we are blessed in the providence of God, and we are blessed in the grace of God.

Now the grace of God is what will give you inward strength to endure. It will give you the wisdom and the stamina to obey Him. When God's call to duty comes, you often feel you can't do it. Of course, that's not really surprising because there are many things in the natural world we can't do. We're asked to undertake something, and we find dismay in our hearts because we feel it's impossible. But we're blessed in grace. God gives us by His goodness inward strength to follow along in His will.

All of this is seen very clearly in the history of Israel. God did things for His people that they couldn't have done for themselves. He gave them a cloud to watch over them by day and a fire to watch over them by night. In all of their traveling, they had never been over this road before, but He didn't give them a map that would enable them to figure out where they were. He did not put it up to them to plan their course. He gave them a cloud in the daytime, and told them to walk when the cloud moved and to stay under the cloud. At night He gave them a pillar of fire, and they stayed in the light no matter what else was going on. They had no idea where they were going next, but whichever way the cloud or the fire moved, that is the way they moved. Their responsibility was not to check the road; their responsibility was to see the cloud and to see the fire and follow it. They were to be ready and willing to move. You cannot have anything like guidance if you do not have people willing to move. Unbelievers have no assurance of guidance. They have to do the best they can for themselves. That is why when unbelievers feel guilty they feel alienated from God. They have to hide out because of their guilt. You can find that unbelievers have a sense of alienation from God, darkened in their own mind, uncertain in their own ignorance, and frightened in their own solitude. When anyone accepts Jesus Christ as Savior and Lord and commits the keeping of his soul to God, he can live with assurance in the midst of everything that is going on because he has been pardoned. No matter what the situation is and what the score against us is, "Though your sins be as scarlet, they shall be as white as snow; though they be red like crimson, they shall be as wool." This is the promise that has been given to us by God. We are assured and pardoned.

Then too, believers are illuminated by revelation from God. That's what Bible study does for you. Bible study will actually open your heart and mind so that you can follow and know the will of God. You may not know the road, but you know who is taking you along the way. You may not know where the road is going to lead and what's going to happen, but you do know God, and He will watch over you. You are comforted by His presence, because He is with you at all times. He will never leave you or forsake you.

This was Israel's experience. In addition to having the cloud and the fire, they had even more. They had faithful leaders, such as Moses and later Joshua, and these men interpreted the guidance of God. It's true that the cloud and fire were seen by everybody, but just when they should move and when they should stop was interpreted for them by leaders who used trumpets to signal the message to the people.

Today we have the Scriptures—the words of the apostles and the prophets—and we have the words of pastors and teachers, and all of these things are given to us to guide us.And our responsibility in this whole matter is to be ready and willing to follow Him. This requires on our part that we should be humble, and we should be yielded to Him. We will be interested to see as we go along in the history of Israel when the people of God lost their joy and their power, and we want to see *why* they did and what we need to do so we won't lose *our* power today.

Do you realize how important it is for things to be done in orderly fashion? "Moreover I will appoint a place for my people Israel, and will plant them, that they may dwell in a place of their own, and move no more; neither shall the children of wickedness afflict them any more, as beforetime" (2 Samuel 7:10). These words are the beginning of a great promise that God made to David and through David to His people. It was a promise that He would bring order into their affairs.

The Covenant with David

Of all the people in the world, only a few have accepted the Lord Jesus Christ. Only a few believe the Gospel and are committed to God. The world calls them Christians, and they're commonly thought of as the people of God. Wherever you see a church you recognize these are some of the people who worship God and in a certain sense belong to Him. They make a profession of faith, and the world calls them Christians. But in this series of studies, we are finding in the Old Testament history of Israel that the people of God can be enslaved. Normally we think of Christians, the people of God, as being victorious. You would expect them to be strong. You would expect them to be free. Yet it is possible for such people to be in defeat and in bondage. When we speak of souls in prison, we speak of the souls of believing people. People who really and truly believe in God can be frightened; people who actually go through the exercises of prayer have no confidence in God. They really believe that they belong to God, yet they're afraid of tomorrow.

Well, there's something wrong, and they're not enjoying the full effect of their faith. We will see this illustrated in the history of Israel when a foreign nation, Babylon, destroyed the city of God, Jerusalem. But just for the present we want to emphasize even more the blessings that the people of God enjoy. So far in our studies, we have noticed that God's people receive blessing as a gift; they don't have to work for blessing. They are reconciled to God by a Substitute; they don't have to pay for the debts they have incurred. And we have noticed also that they are led along the way by God Himself.

These people are to have a kingdom established for them. Now that word "kingdom" is not so commonly used with us today, but I think we can understand it. The essence of a kingdom is the king, because the king is the one who directs the activity of those in his kingdom. The presence of a king in a country means there is order out of chaos. With everything in confusion and mixed up in turmoil, the king will establish order and bring things into proper arrangement.

I wonder if you recognize the blessing there is in this. When you hear, for example, that God will bless His people, do you know what that blessing means? One thing, of course, that the blessing means is that they will have fellowship with God. They'll be reconciled to Him. But I want you to see another aspect of that blessing —that He will bring order into their lives. We can understand what it's like when we have confusion —everything going pell-mell, people going helter-skelter, running into one another all the time. Then you have contention—people fussing with one another. You have conflict. If you brought order into a situation like that, the result would be peace, and peace would be a great blessing. When a person's activities are scattered, interests are scattered. He does this today, but he'll do the opposite tomorrow. He gives himself over this way now and that way next time. There is weakness in this, but if you could bring in order and get everything moving in the same direction at the same time, you would have strength.

The same is true with reference to one's feeling about things. When you have confusion—turmoil, everybody saying everything, this way, that way, the other way, no way—if you have this brought into order, you are getting guidance. Someone takes charge and directs. I suppose the most commonplace way we would see this would be in a traffic situation. Can you imagine the difficulty we'd experience in our cities if we did not have traffic control? Or think of activity on an athletic field. If you had a group of folks on an athletic field or in a gymnasium doing whatever they wanted to do, you'd have utter confusion. But if you organize a game and get it under control, bring in an umpire or a referee, then you have something that gets to be interesting. The same situation happens in an office. You can't have an office where nobody knows for sure what to do. Some things would be left undone; some things would be done over the second time. What you need is someone in control—an office manager. The same thing is true in the schoolroom. You can have all the children there in their desks, and you can have all the books open before them, and they may know enough to do something with them. But the odds are that they won't do anything unless you have a teacher—someone who will take charge. This is true also in a family. If you have a family in which no one is in charge, and nobody's voice is the controlling voice, then you have contention and confusion.

I wonder how often you've suffered distress because you didn't know for sure what to do with your money, and you had more bills to pay than you could handle. You have more things to want than you can pay for. And what is it you need? It's pretty elementary—you need a budget. The moment you bring in a budget you say, "This comes first; that comes next. If there's anything left over, then I can have that." And you can budget your time, too. Each of us has the same amount of time, yet some of us seem to have no time at all. What's our problem? Well, you bring in a schedule. Just like you have a *budget* for finances, you have a *schedule* for time. You have a *program* for work. This is the essence of order—a place for everything and everything in its place.

Now you might ask what that has to do with Christian life. Well, if you have your heart and mind given over to the Lord Jesus Christ, He has a way of disposing you to put first things first. And if you put first things first, that begins to establish order.

How will God bring this kind of blessing into your life? What you need is a guide. You need someone who will work in you like a director. All the music that the choir is going to sing may be well written and nicely printed, and you have it there in your music folio, but the choir will need a director. But you ask, "If I'm going to have the Lord Jesus Christ be the Lord of my life, do I have any part in it at all?" Yes, all the way through the part you play is keeping the rules. You do what you're told. There needs to be obedience, and we need to be humble about rendering it. The peace that comes into the heart as a result of accepting Jesus as Lord brings quietness and rest and strength. And Christian people, the people of God, can actually have the inward guidance and be led along in the things of the Lord. If Christians become nervous or flustered or bewildered, it just means that the kingdom has not really been established in their hearts.

Do you feel that you know what the word "grace" means? "For by grace are ye saved through faith." That's the way the Apostle Paul wrote it in Ephesians 2:8. He's speaking of the grace of God.

In this country there is plenty of evidence that there are Christians. You can look around and see the church buildings. You can hear popular hymns over the radio and on television. You know about the *The Mercy of God* great evangelists that come to town and hold meetings. Everybody knows that some people are Christians. The world may not have a very clear idea of who they are, or why they are, but they all know *that* they are.

In previous chapters we've discussed some of the blessings that Christians have. We have pointed out that one of the Christian's blessings is the fact that everything he receives is a gift from God. He doesn't work for it. The Christian himself is reconciled to God because someone else paid the price. So far as the Christian is concerned, he is blessed because he is led every day by the hand of God in his affairs. The affairs of Christians are ordered into quiet and peacefulness by the Lord our Guide. But I want you to see one more great blessing that the people of God have. God shows grace toward them, and grace has been well defined as the undeserved kindness and favor of God toward man.

There's one Old Testament incident that illustrates this perfectly—found in 2 Samuel 9. The background of this story has to do with the early life of David. You will remember that while David was a boy on his father's farm, King Saul was a great man, but a failure in the eyes of God. Samuel went out to the farm and anointed David to be king. So David is anointed to be king in place of Saul, but David is just a poor country boy. He comes to the king to take part in the battle against the Philistines, and he is enabled by the grace of God to kill the great giant, Goliath. So David becomes a prominent person.

Now Saul also had a son, Jonathan, who greatly loved David and helped him. And as Jonathan and David battled together, Jonathan knew that David would become king in his place. He said to David, "I know that by the will of God you are going to become king in my place. I'll help you in every way I possibly can, but I want you to do one thing for me. When you do get to be king, I wish that you would treat my family with kindness." And David promised that he would do this. And so in the course of time, David was made king. Before he came to the throne, both Saul and Jonathan were killed in battle. After long and prolonged civil war—seven years of fighting with the house of Saul—David was finally established on the throne of all Israel. Then he remembered he had promised Jonathan he would take care of his family. So he raised the question, "Is there yet any that is left of the house of Saul, that I may shew him kindness for Jonathan's sake?" And they brought in a son of Jonathan's by the name of Mephibosheth. All we're told about him is that he was "lame on his feet," which is to say he was a cripple. Mephibosheth is brought before the king. There had been war between the house of David and the house of Saul, and Mephibosheth was Saul's grandson. So he is now an alien. He has been defeated in battle; he is like a prisoner of war. All his property has been confiscated. This man is brought before the king. When David recognizes who he is, that this is actually Jonathan's son, he orders, "Restore his property." He stipulates that there will always be a place at his table for Mephibosheth. And so this lame, crippled son of Jonathan is brought in to sit at the king's table for the rest of his days.

This is a demonstration of the grace of God. Mephibosheth, the crippled son of Jonathan, is actually the grandson of Saul and on the opposite side from David, the king. But David takes this man, brings him into his presence, restores all the property he had lost in battle, and treats him as the king's son. He is given a place at the king's table, and he is to sit there the rest of his days. And then the Bible says about him, that he was lame in his feet.

Do you see how much I am like Mephibosheth? The Lord Jesus Christ came into this world for me. He came into this world to die on behalf of sinners, and after He had died, God raised Him from the dead. And after He was raised from the dead, He ascended into Heaven. And there He was glorified, and there He sits at the right hand of God. He came to show the grace of God to me. I'm one of those who caused His death. My sin was actually one of the reasons why He had to die. Because of my sin, I was actually, in a sense, at war with Him. Yet He died for me. And now that my sin has been recognized I'm called into the very presence of God. I am not righteous, not a single bit, in the presence of God. Yet

God bestows upon me all that I had ever lost in my sin, and treats me as one of His own. He gives me a place at the King's table. "Beloved, behold what manner of love the Father hath bestowed upon us, that we should be called the children of God." This is what is given to the Christian. This is the way with the people of God. And you could very well ask yourself a question like this: could such blessed persons, so graciously favored of God, ever fall into neglect? Could they ever be defeated?

The
Word
of God

Do you realize that all our hopes rest upon promises? "All the promises of God are yea and amen in Christ Jesus." That is the way it is written in the New Testament. And that would encourage us in everything that we look to God about. The people of God are distinguished from all other people in the world by what they're expecting God to do. It doesn't mean that the people of God are better than other people. It

The Promises of God

doesn't mean that the people of God are smarter, or that they're purer, or that they're stronger. The people of God are distinguished in their faith, by what they are expecting God to do.

There are many people who do not believe in God in the Gospel sense. They may believe there is a God, but they're not really putting any trust in Him. They're not really counting on Him. It's a lonely, benighted existence that many people live. They've got no help anywhere, and that means they've got no hope. Deep down in their own hearts, they know right well they're not strong enough—not good enough. Many people are not believers in God. When they look ahead, they think of what they intend to do, and then they settle for a certain expectation. If that expectation is optimistic, they think they can manage it if they just work hard. If it's a depressing expectation, they will live in dread, and that's when deep down in their hearts they say, "What's the use? It just doesn't matter."

With the people who belong to God, it's entirely different. And by the way, anybody could belong. "Whosoever will, let him come." Brother, you can't get it any simpler than that. And you know that puts the responsibility right where it belongs. A person either will or he won't. And if he will, he can come; and if he won't, he can't. Those who do come know what God will do for His people. They've heard the voice of the Lord Jesus say, "Come unto me all ye that labor and are heavy laden, and I will give you rest." And they believed that He meant them personally. You see this is the invitation given abroad to anybody. Whosoever is "heavy laden" let him come. And the Lord Jesus promises, "I will give you rest."

When people believe this call, and when they have come, then they've become people of God. That's what we mean by this phrase, and these are the folks we're going to talk about. I want you to know a little bit more about the assurances that they have, because of the promises of God. I told you that our hopes rest upon promises. If you're hoping for something tomorrow, you haven't been there yet. You don't know what will happen.

What are you hoping to do tomorrow? Are you hoping to go about your work in your house? In other words, you know the house isn't going to burn down—or blow up. You're going to be healthy and well. You won't break a leg, and you won't be paralyzed. Don't you see what you're hoping? You're hoping you'll be like you are; you're hoping the house will be like it is, and you're hoping other people will be like they are. Everything you see gives a certain promise in a natural way of what you can expect tomorrow. Your hopes are based upon what you've figured out is going to happen. That's what I mean by the promise of the thing.

If I look at a chair, you know what I think is going to happen if I sit on it? I think it's going to hold me up. That's the promise of the chair. The very fact that it's standing there in the house, right there by the table, promises it will hold me up if I sit on it. Now if it breaks down, it didn't keep its promise and I just got fooled. When you get in your car, that car promises, everything else being all right, that if you turn on the ignition key the car will start. That's what it promises.

People of God have certain things that they expect from God because He said He would do it. For instance, they know that God at one time said, "I will never leave thee nor forsake thee." They cherish that. Just think of what it would mean to you if you knew that the Lord Jesus Christ would say, "I will never leave thee nor forsake thee." Don't you see how you could rest in that? You may have burdens and you may have problems, and you may have to face things today that are different from anything you have ever had to face before, and you may be in trouble right now such as you've never seen before. But you have the word of the Lord Jesus Christ that He will never leave you. "I will hold thee by thy right hand." Think of it! This is what God has to say to you. "I will guide thee with mine eye," the way a mother guides her child while she's watching over it. And she's watching it all the time. This is the promise of God.

Do you realize that if you belong to God, you'll never

get away from Him? He isn't going to forget you. He'll
always be right there with you to do you good. Or listen
to this promise. "Whosoever cometh unto me, I will in
no wise cast out." I expect one reason why I like that one
so much is that it lets me in for sure, because I did come
to Him, and I did put my trust in Him, and I'm counting
on Him to do what He said He would do.

Jesus promised, "I am the door; by me if any man
enter in, he shall be saved." There it is, just as plain as
day. "I am the way, the truth and the life. No man
cometh unto the Father but by me." Now listen to
another promise: "Though your sins be as scarlet, they
shall be as white as snow; though they be red like crimson, they shall be as wool." And I think of another one
from the New Testament: "The blood of Jesus Christ His
Son, cleanseth us from all sin." The blood of Jesus Christ
His Son already has been shed—already a matter of
record and of history. There's another promise that
you'll find in 1 John 2:1 that reads like this: "If any man
sin, we have an advocate with the Father, Jesus Christ
the righteous." Think of the assurance that gives you.
You're not going to sin if you can help it. You don't want
to. But if you do, you won't be gone. There will be
Someone watching over you and keeping you.

Then listen to the words of the Lord Jesus Christ:
"Whosoever therefore shall confess me before men, him
will I confess also before my Father which is in heaven."
Stand up in front of people and let them know that you
really do believe. You don't have to say you are going to
be good. You don't have to say you are going to be
perfect. You only need to testify openly that you do

believe in the Lord Jesus Christ. Then think of this as a promise: "He that hath begun a good work in you will complete it." Isn't that wonderful? You're going to be taken care of. These are His promises. "I will not leave you comfortless." Or again, "If you ask anything in my name, I will do it." Or listen to this: "Nothing shall by any means hurt you." Oh, I could go on and on with the promises that are given to you in Christ Jesus. The whole consciousness of a Christian is illuminated by these precious promises. It's a wonderful thing to belong to the Lord Jesus Christ.

Would you understand why a sinner would need someone to represent him and to intercede for him with God?
"For every high priest taken from among men is or-
dained for men in things pertaining to God, that he may
offer both gifts and sacrifices for sins" (Hebrews 5:1).
Of all the blessings which
God has provided for His
people, there's nothing
more comforting than the
assurance that we have a
merciful High Priest.

The Priest

This word, "priest," is variously used in common
speech, but I'm going to have to ignore the common
usage and bring it to you the way the New Testament
uses it. We must be sure to understand the Bible meaning. The word, "priest," doesn't mean wearing a certain
kind of uniform. It's not having on a certain type of
clothes. It's not even going through certain perform-
ances, connected with certain religious rites and cere-
monies. The word, "priest," is a functional word; there
is something a priest is supposed to *do*. He is supposed
to represent the sinner to God. He is to be toward God
for the sinner like my lawyer is toward the judge for me
while I'm in court. Coming to God involves much that
needs to be learned, because the sinner has broken
God's law; and yet he comes to be accepted as a welcome
worshipper. The sinner who would turn to God actually
has guilt. He's done wrong, and more than that he's
unclean. In fact, a sinner might easily come to God with
just one thing in mind—that he personally doesn't want
to go to hell.

You'll need to have more than that. The people God is going to receive are those who look into His face and are willing to accept His way of doing things. But God's "way" can't be figured out by just anybody. It isn't a question of people getting together somewhere and figuring out what would be a good way to please God. You'll find one kind of worship going on in Africa, and another kind of worship going on in Asia, and another kind of worship going on among North American Indians, and all these various kinds of worship are human ideas of how to do it. But men didn't have to think up the idea of turning to God. If man feels there is a God, then man wants to get to Him, believe me! If God can help a man, if there is any balm in Gilead, if there's any way of getting any help for the state that he's in, then the man wants it. So the sinner desperately tries to find out how to come to God. There is a way to do it, a way that takes into account all the realities that are involved. But there are many things that a sinner can't know. Instead of being left to grope in darkness, to experiment in ignorance about things, the sinner is provided a Guide. "If any man sin, we have an advocate with the Father, even Jesus Christ the righteous."

Now, anybody can join this company; anybody can become a Christian. You can become one of the people of God. It's an open invitation: "Come unto Me," and anybody who comes will receive what Jesus has for him.

But for those who are trusting in the Lord Jesus Christ already, it is important for you to realize what He does for us when He acts as our Priest. The best example is the lawyer in the court room. But actually there are two aspects of this truth, and I want to consider both of them. The first is that Christ Jesus is spoken of as our *High* Priest. That means He's the head of all the priests. Of all the people who intercede for us, He is the Chief Intercessor. He more than anybody else, represents us to His Father and prays for us.

Keep in mind, please, that Christ Jesus has a good standing before God. He can come before the Father openly because He is Jesus Christ the Righteous. He has done everything that He ought to do. Keep in mind, too, that the Father loves the Son and commits all things into His hands. With the Lord Jesus Christ representing us, and going into the presence of God, we are in good hands. Because the beloved Lord Jesus is acceptable to God, the Father has made us acceptable "in the Beloved." The Lord Jesus knows the holiness of God; He knows the penalty of sin; He knows the righteousness of God; He knows what it takes to keep the economy of God's law and God's justice straightened out.

Many people who have never considered what is involved can easily think to themselves, "If God wanted to, He could just forgive." That's just like saying that if man wanted to, he could forgive every debt that's on his books. That would be a good way to go bankrupt. Sooner or later someone is going to have to pay up. With God there will be a day when the showdown actually does come. And knowing that, Jesus Christ comes to me, and I receive Him as my Savior. He takes His place as my High Priest. He represents me before God. He comes into the presence of God, knowing all that is involved, and when He comes in, He's got what it takes to get me forgiven. He has His own blood that He shed for me. And He comes and presents it to the Father, and He presents it on my behalf.

Another thing that you can keep in mind when you think about Christ Jesus being our High Priest, is that He understands our situation. When He became incarnate and He came into this world and was found in fashion as a man, He tasted all the experiences of life and death that you and I have. He is touched with all the feelings of our infirmities. Having been tempted in all points as we are, and yet without sin, He understands us—He is sympathetic. You must remember when you're thinking about Jesus of Nazareth, that He is the One who is standing at the graveside of Lazarus, knowing full well He was going to raise Lazarus from the dead. Yet when He saw the grief of Mary and Martha, we read that "Jesus wept." The Lord Jesus is a compassionate friend.

The third thing I want to emphasize is that compassion. He actually looks upon us with mercy and He really wants to help us out. Time and again in Matthew, Mark, Luke and John, you'll read how the Lord Jesus met sinners. Do you remember any time that He had any disposition to reject anybody because that man or that woman was a sinner? No, He always welcomed them. This was not because he approved of their sin, for He didn't. But He could cleanse that. It was not because He liked the condition that they were in. He could change that.

But now there is another thing I want to tell you about the priesthood, and that is that the believer himself is to be a priest. The Lord Jesus Christ is our *High* Priest, but every Christian person is a priest. He is to intercede on behalf of his loved ones, and on behalf of other people. The Christian person should always exercise himself in prayer for other people whenever he has opportunity to do it. It's a wonderful thing to keep one verse in mind when we're thinking about the Priesthood of the Lord Jesus Christ: "But this man, because he continueth ever, hath an unchangeable priesthood. Wherefore he is able also to save them to the uttermost that come unto God by him, seeing he ever liveth to make intercession for them" (Hebrews 7:24-25). This means He can save us all the way through, starting now and on to the end, every day, every month of the year, and as long as we live. Isn't it a wonderful thing that we have Him on our side, and that He is interceding for us in the presence of God?

Do you think people could understand the Bible without a preacher? "And he gave some, apostles; and some, prophets; and some, evangelists; and some, pastors and teachers; for the perfecting of the saints, for the work of the ministry, for the edifying of the body of Christ" (Ephesians 4:11-12). These words were written by the Apostle Paul when he was describing the Christian church. He was saying that Almighty God through the

The Prophet

Holy Spirit has given to the church certain gifts to enable the church to grow and prosper and be useful. And he said some of these gifts are apostles, prophets, evangelists, pastors and teachers.

When you stop and think about it, this means that so far as the believers are concerned it was not expected that they would always find out for themselves what the will of God is. Actually they had the Scriptures even at the time of Paul. They had the Old Testament, and they had the traditions of the church—the spoken message of the Gospel as it was given out by the apostles. But the Apostle Paul did not think of the Christians of his day and time finding out for themselves what the will of God would be, even though they had the Old Testament Scriptures and the witness of the people who had seen Jesus Christ raised from the dead. They needed help —the kind of help that an apostle would give, or a pastor or teacher—and for that reason, God provided these people for that purpose. Now look in 1 Corinthians 14:3. "But he that prophesieth speaketh unto men to edification, and exhortation, and comfort." For the word, "prophesieth," you can put the word, "preaches," in its place. That makes it say, "He that preaches does it so men might be built up in edification, encouraged in exhortation, and comforted." And this is what God has done for them.

One reason why it is hard for people to understand the Christian Gospel is because it deals with invisible things. Of course, Christians live in a visible world. It's where they sleep and where they wake up in the morning and where they eat breakfast and where they wash and hang out their clothes. Christians do live in this world, whether they recognize the fact or not. If a Christian's going to be kind, he's going to be kind in this world. And if a Christian is going to be good, it's got to be right here in this world. These things happen right here.

But the faith of a Christian reaches "beyond the veil." It reaches beyond the senses into the invisible. A Christian's faith reaches into what he cannot see. And part of the problem of understanding the Gospel is that the Gospel itself involves eternal things. Paul puts it like this: "The things which are seen are temporal, but the things which are not seen are eternal."

So there is the big difference between that which is of this world, temporal, and that which is of the other world, everlasting. Many other religions in the world teach things that people have figured out for themselves; the Christian believes what has been revealed by God. It is necessary in the very nature of things to have a revelation from God if we're going to understand the eternal. When the Bible raises the question, "Who by searching can find out God?" the answer is, nobody. You wouldn't know where to look and you wouldn't know what to think if you saw God. It is possible, of course, for God to show Himself, and in the history of the people of God, He has done that. God reveals Himself in nature all around us—and that's one of the first things you think about when someone mentions God. He's the One who makes the flowers, and He's the One who makes the birds, and He's the One who puts the mountains in their places. It's true that nature reveals God. The Bible puts it this way: "The heavens declare the glory of God; and the firmament showeth his handiwork" (Psalm 19:1). You could look into nature and learn something about God.

But God reveals Himself also in providence, in the way things happen. That this thing happens to you and not that thing shows the sovereignty of God. God reveals Himself also in the conscience of man, for man in his own inward being senses some things are right and some things are wrong. Paul says that man shows the work of the law of God in his own heart when his thoughts either accuse or excuse him. All of these things—nature, providence and conscience—will help a man recognize himself and see himself as God sees him. And I'll tell you one thing man will see: he's a sinner in the sight of God. Everything you see in nature is true, but nature can destroy you. You can drown in a lake —and that's a part of nature. Fire can burn your house down—that's a part of nature. Everything you see in nature is true, everything you see in providence is important, and everything you can feel in your conscience is valid. But it doesn't go far enough to save your soul. If you knew everything about nature, everything about providence, everything about conscience, you'd still be lost. That's why God reveals more. He reveals His grace through the Scriptures. "The law of the Lord is perfect, converting the soul."

In an earlier chapter we referred to the fact that the people of God have the promises of God. Now those promises of God go beyond the natural process. God promised to do things for you beyond nature because these things come out of His grace, and these promises need to be understood. Not everyone receives direct communication from God. Some people think that if ideas come to them and they have a whole plan of activity come to them, that this is from God. Not necessarily! John writes, "Beloved, believe not every spirit, but try the spirits whether they are of God: because many false prophets are gone out into the world" (1 John 4:1). God makes Himself known only to a few people—not to everybody. And the Bible speaks of them as prophets.It says, "God, who at sundry times and in divers manners spake in time past unto the fathers by the prophets" (Hebrews 1:1). So God then does send prophets to declare His Word. 2 Peter 1:21 tells us, "For the prophecy came not in old time by the will of man: but holy men of God spake as they were moved by the Holy Ghost." God revealed His will to some people in a special way and these people could explain it to others. Deuteronomy 5:27-29 refers to a time when Moses was dealing with the children of Israel, and the children of Israel speak: "Go thou near," they said to Moses, "and hear all that the Lord our God shall say: and speak thou unto us all that the Lord our God shall speak unto thee; and we will hear it, and do it." And Moses goes on to say that "The Lord heard the voice of your words, when ye spake unto me; and the Lord said unto me, I have heard the voice of the words of this people, which they have spoken unto thee: they have well said all that they have spoken." That was the arrangement. God would speak to Moses, and Moses would speak to the people. That's where the prophet comes in. You see, in the Scripture, there are covenants—promises that God has made known. He made known a certain promise to Abraham, and we to this day depend upon that Covenant with Abraham. He made known a certain promise to David, and we to this day rejoice in the Covenant with David. It gives us the assurance that it's the will of God for Christ Jesus, the seed of David, to be on the throne forever. A prophet is one who tells us about these things. The prophet is the one who interprets the history of God's people to us and shows us what it means. The prophet takes the Scriptures and opens them up to show us what these things mean. God's people have His revelation ministered to them by His prophets, and that is one of the blessings they enjoy.

Under what circumstances do you feel a person would need to be directed? "For unto us a child is born, unto us a son is given: and the government shall be upon his shoulder: and his name shall be called Wonderful, Counselor, The mighty God, The everlasting Father, The Prince of Peace. Of the increase of his government and peace there shall be no end, upon the throne of David, and upon his kingdom, to order it, and establish it with judgment and with justice from henceforth even for ever" Isaiah 9:6-7). This is an Old Testament prophecy, and everyone who reads it understands that this points forward to the coming of the Messiah, whom we call Christ. It is said of Christ Jesus that "the government shall be upon his shoulder."

The King

You know, whether we're Christian or not Christian, one of our most frustrating experiences is to be bewildered by so many choices. There are so many different directions we could go—so many different things we could be doing. We've got five dollars, and there are so many different ways we could spend it. And this is frustrating. But if you get a group of people together, wondering what they're going to do, it's even worse. If you're going to have a group do anything, that requires group direction. Someone must be in charge and tell them what to do. Now the value of this can be seen in every direction that you look. If you went into a store and found a whole staff of clerks and workers with no management, if there wasn't somebody who was responsible to direct their activity, you'd have inefficiency all around.

Human beings, you know, are marked by their interest in variety. The Book of Isaiah says, "We have turned every one to his own way; and the Lord hath laid on him the iniquity of us all." It says, "All we like sheep have gone astray." This is characteristic of all mankind. As sure as you have three people together, you have three different ideas. You have at least three different judgments, and you're going to have three different choices. Everyone of us needs somehow or other inwardly to establish a control because of the various ideas that come to our mind. It's a natural thing for human beings to have random activity, going in all directions. If I want to know what human nature is really like, I go and watch a baby lying on its back. That's where you'll see random activity—the two arms and the two legs go in at least four different directions. They need to be brought under control before that child can walk. Before that child can handle anything, he needs to gain control of his muscles. Each part needs to be subject to the central authority.

For the benefit of everybody, random activity has to be disciplined and put under control. In Old Testament times, when the people of God came together as a group, this control was secured several different ways. First of all, it came by the Ten Commandments. The law of God united the people and brought them together around God's standards. Then again, they had the worship of God in the Tabernacle. They all came to the altar; they all brought their sacrifices; they were brought before God by prayer of the Priest; and they were brought together by their various leaders. In the days when Moses was a leader, he was the leader of everybody. When Joshua was the leader, he was the leader of everybody. And then when the Judges came along, each one of them in turn had a whole company of people following him. And so it was afterwards when they had the king. When the king was a good king and a strong king, he was the king of everybody.

That was the plan, then, to bring random activity in the nation under control and have it work together to one end. But this plan was not carried out completely or perfectly. And one reason was because the people in Israel simply did not want to do as they were directed to do. They wanted to go their own private way—their own selfish way. And because Israel was incorrigible about this, one way or another they would do what they wanted to do in their own way, and afterwards come to grief. Whenever Israel prospered, it was when central control was operative. It was when all the people got together, made Saul king, and followed him, that they won the victory. Success in Old Testament times came when central control was operative.

Now the New Testament comes at it in a different way. The New Testament is based on new birth, and the new birth means that individual people are going to have a new nature. You had military leaders in the Old Testament, and prophets who told about the Word of God, and Priests who guided the people in their worship of God. You had all these leaders, but you didn't have the disposition to do the will of God. "All we like sheep have

gone astray; we have turned every one to his own way."
The children of Israel had sinned before God, and even if
they were forgiven, they couldn't go on that way. So
God promised He would make a different arrangement
in the New Covenant. Direction would be in the hands
of One who really is the sovereign King, and He would
guide, and He would rule over them all. But naturally
speaking, people don't even have the disposition to do
what that great King wants them to do. So the disposition to do the will of God is the result of the new birth.
It's the new person in Christ Jesus who wants to do the
will of God. That's why when Nicodemus asked the
Lord Jesus to explain what His preaching was all about,
Christ told him "Ye must be born again." It's born again
souls who love the Lord Jesus and are willing to obey
Him. And so this whole truth of the New Testament is
activated in the individual Christian by the indwelling
Holy Spirit of God.

You may have the will of God before you, but how will
you have the disposition to *do* His will? How will you
want to do what He wants done? This is what happens
when a person is born again and receives from God the
Holy Spirit. This whole thing is activated in the individual believer by the indwelling Holy Spirit who pro-
pels the individual into the service of God. God's people
are to be led. Isaiah said, "If ye be willing and obedient,
ye shall eat the good of the land." With his spiritual
welfare at stake, it's the born again soul who willingly
yields to the will of God and is led by the Holy Spirit of
God.

Do you realize that no Christian is authorized to try to solve his own problems? "According to the purpose of him who worketh all things after the counsel of his own will," is the way the Bible describes the Christian life. There are many things in the Gospel that are different from natural life. Some aspects of the Gospel are of such a nature that when men find out what's really involved in becoming a Christian they turn away.

The Purpose of God

The Lord Jesus said, "If any man will be my disciple, let him deny himself, take up his cross and follow me."

It's a very natural thing, of course, to want to do as you please. You see it in every baby, and when the baby grows up, he still wants to do whatever it pleases him to do. But that's not the Christian way. So far as the Christian is concerned, he yields himself into God's hands to accept God's will in his life. But God's control is benevolent. God will keep him from harm, and will lead him in such a way as to bring him into blessing. And the glory of this truth lies in the purpose of God. There is no glory from the human point of view in giving yourself up and yielding yourself. It's not a glorious thing to be involved in something that makes you small in everyone's eyes. But the outcome of it is glorious when we accept the guidance of God and submit to the government of God.

The Bible teaches that the Son of God will be over everything. He will sit on the throne of David and put all the other forces in subjection to Him. The people of God actually belong to this King of Kings, Jesus Christ, of whom it is said, "The government shall be upon his shoulder . . . Of the increase of his government and peace there shall be no end." The people of God share in His glory the way a Queen shares in the glory of her King. The King is the strong one who has control of the government, and who directs the affairs of state, and the Queen is his bride. She loves him and rejoices in him, and she helps him in any way she can. The people of God have in their experience this blessedness, that they walk with the King.

Now, so far as the individual Christian is concerned, it's also glorious. "And we know that all things work together for good to them that love God, to them who are the called according to his purpose" (Romans 8:28). Every single event in the life and in the experience of the Christian will promote the will of God. God is able to make each circumstance good for His own purposes. God isn't just going to make it easy for me to live out my life. He is going to make it so that I will live out *His* life. This is the significance of yielding ourselves to Him.

When someone suggests that man is supposed to solve the problems of the world, I feel like saying, "Isn't it an amazing thing that we can forget so quickly!" You see, God will take care of the things of this world in His own time, and He'll do it the way He wants to do it. The Christian is not here to try to find solutions to the world's problems. Jesus said, "The Son can do nothing of himself. My Father worketh hitherto, and I work." All He wanted was to have things done as His Father in Heaven wanted them done. "My Father doeth the work," He said. The Christian will accept the situation he is in as being from God. If we leave matters in His hands, He can work things out for His own glory, and this is something that you and I need to remember all the time. The people of God have all these promises of God on their behalf, and God plans to bless them and to enrich them.

Now in these chapters we've been speaking of some of the benefits that the people of God have. We have tried to identify the people of God so we can know who it is we're talking about. We've found out that even when the children of Israel were in the spot where God wanted them to be, that God still had in mind to lead them. He had given them a promise that would draw them nearer to Himself. He had given them a priest that would help them. He had given them a prophet that would teach them. And He had also given them a King that would direct them into effective service. In other words, to be one of the people of God means that you've got many things going for you, because God has a purpose in everything that is happening, and He wants to lead you along in His ways.

Now we've taken time to consider all these things because in the next chapter we're going to see the children of Israel come to a very strange experience. We're going to find the children of Israel actually turning away from God in spite of all that had been done for them. I want us to see that people who turn away from God can be even the fortunate people who have been saved and blessed. In Old Testament days, the work that was done for the people was done in the natural world. God called the children of Israel out of the land of Egypt to come across the desert into the land of Canaan. That was done in this world and through the natural processes. But it was God who was providing for them and taking care of them and leading them into the land He had provided. He would take them into the land, and He would give it to them, but there was one condition: they were to keep His Word and do His will. And we find out when we read the Old Testament that man naturally is not disposed to do the will of God. In spite of everything that's done for him, he still tends to do it his own way, and that is what the children of Israel did. And because they did it that way, they passed through a period of captivity. Just because a person is a Christian doesn't mean that he's become perfect. Just because you're a believer doesn't mean that you've become an angel.

You need the help of God, but you have found out that God will give it to you. He will give you the strength and the wisdom you need. He will provide for you, and you can trust Him fully, but you need Him. His purpose to lead us into His will can never be completed if we do it in our own strength. We need the help of God in everything that we do.

*The Sin
of
His People*

Have you ever realized how natural it is for us to drop out of relationships that are beneficial to us? "For my people have committed two evils; they have forsaken me the fountain of living waters, and hewed them out cisterns, broken cisterns, that can hold no water." These words that are recorded in the Book of Jeremiah—the complaint that God made about His people. The people of God are capable of acting very foolishly.

Forsaking God

They can turn away from God and enter into a time when their experience is clouded, and they're not really being blessed.

It's very important to remember that just because a person belongs to God does not mean he is different in himself. If a person was inclined to be foolish at the time he put his trust in the Lord Jesus Christ, he's still inclined to be foolish as a Christian—at least, naturally speaking. Now in Christ Jesus you *can* become different. But unless you grow and become different, the way you *were* is the way you will go on being. Let's put it like this. If you were a strong person and you were wading through a muddy bog and you came to a rock, you could stand on the rock safely and securely in all your strength. If you were a weak person and you were wading through the mud and you came upon the rock, you could stand on the rock faithfully, but you'd still be a weak person. Your situation would be different because of the rock, but your condition would be the same.

I think you will see this better if you consider what happens when a person gets married. Here's a young woman who is not inclined to be careful about her things—she's not a neat person. Probably she dreams that if she gets married everything will change, but it won't. She'll be the same person after she gets married that she was before. Her experience will be different, and I hope she'll be happier, but she'll be what she was. What I mean to say is that if people have in them the capacity to turn away from God, they can still do it as Christians. I know this may sound discouraging, but it's true; and because it's true we need to be careful about it.

Now someone may say, "Do you really think it would ever be possible for God's people to turn away from God?" Well go right up to the very summit and consider the apostolic company, and find out what happened to them. There were twelve apostles, and one of them turned away—a traitor. Judas was in with the Lord Jesus for three years, but he was a human being, and that's what a human being can do. Let's take the example of a husband and wife. They were in love with each other and got married and lived together for a long time. Do you think it's possible that the husband could ever turn away from his wife, or the wife from her husband? And what of the child that is growing up in the home and loves its mother and its father? Do you think it's possible that when the child gets to be a teenager he can turn away from home? In each case the answer is yes! It is possible. Husbands turn away from their wives; wives turn away from their husbands. Children neglect their parents. People can foolishly turn away from God.

Do you feel it could never happen with a Christian? Look at Hebrews 3:12: "Take heed, brethren, lest there be in any of you an evil heart of unbelief, in departing from the living God." This is not said to unbelievers —people of the world. It's talking about God's people, and I'm writing now about those who do the foolish thing of departing from God. Someone may say, "Well after you once came to know Jesus Christ, you wouldn't do it then. You wouldn't ever turn away from the Lord Jesus." But look at John 6:66: "From that time many of his disciples went back, and walked no more with him." They departed from Him. Now how could this ever happen? Well, how is it possible that the husband who really loved the girl when he married her take her for granted? How could that ever be?

"Hath a nation changed their gods, which are yet no gods?" Jeremiah asks. "But my people have changed their glory for that which doth not profit. Be astonished, O ye heavens, at this, and be horribly afraid, be ye very desolate, saith the Lord. For my people have committed two evils; they have forsaken me the fountain of living waters, and hewed them out cisterns, broken cisterns, that can hold no water." I hope you can see the danger here. There was nothing wrong with the fact that Israel wanted water. God never had any objection to that. But do you know what they did? They made great big containers that they could gather the water and keep it in, instead of depending upon the fountain where the fresh water was coming out. To put it in spiritual terms, they wanted the blessing, but they didn't want the Lord.

There are any number of people who want the blessing of God but don't want to have fellowship with Jesus Christ. They can talk about Jesus Christ as a character in history—as a teacher or as an example. But to talk about Jesus Christ as a living Person, and to have dealings with Him as Lord and Master is something else. Yes indeed—people want the blessing of God; they want the peace and the joy; they want His providence; but they don't want any bother connected with it. They're like people who want all the benefits of married life but they don't want the complications that go with the marriage commitment. "They have forsaken me the fountain of living water." If Israel had stayed in fellowship with God, He would have blessed them day by day. Living water, of course, means running water. There is a great difference between water that is running and water that is standing stagnant in a pool. Now in Christ Jesus the believer can have a fountain of running water. That kind of water is sweet and clean and wonderful to have, whereas the water that gathers in tanks and barrels can be very stagnant. That's the kind of water Israel claimed as its own when the people turned away from the fountain of living water, and hewed them out cisterns.

Do you know that your inclinations today are pretty well what they have been for human beings through the centuries? "And they forsook the Lord and served Baal and Ashtaroth" (Judges 2:13). That's the way Israel is described back in the time of judges. We've been thinking about the people of God who in their peril did something foolish. That's because they could be fooled. There's not much danger of people who

Baal
and
Ashtaroth

know God turning openly against Him. But there's always danger of a person being deceived into accepting something less than the best.

You become a child of God by believing in the Lord Jesus Christ. When you believe in the Lord Jesus Christ, that means you receive Him as your personal Savior. A person becomes a Christian by personally acknowledging before God that he has sinned. Then he believes that Jesus Christ came to die for sinners, and believing that Christ Jesus came to die for him and was buried for him and raised from the dead for him, he enters into this life through faith. The result of belonging to the Lord Jesus Christ and actually having Jesus Christ active in you is blessing. You have peace of heart. You have blessing in the home. You have blessing in your business. You begin to realize that you find this peace of heart when you worship God, and you worship God by going to church, so you go to church. You want your home to be blessed, so you take the family to church and you enter into the church life. You find that when you walk with God you get along in business.

Now it could happen that a person who learns these things starts thinking that peace of mind will come if he goes to church. But just going to church won't do it. Walking into a church building won't change your mind. The peace of mind is worshipping God, and going to church is secondary. Then in order to have blessing in your home you decide you'll have a family altar, and you begin praying in the home. You talk to the Lord and you ask God's blessing. And your home is blessed because you asked Him for it—not just because you had Bible reading and prayer.

Let's examine the home for a minute and use it to understand the principle better. The home started with a courtship. The boy loved the girl and the girl liked the boy and they kept company and finally got married, and then there was a honeymoon. Then they began to set up their home. There were benefits on both sides. The husband had good meals cooked for him, his laundry done, his house kept clean, because he had a wife. But a man can get to where he remembers the cooking and the housekeeping and the laundry and take all the other things for granted. The same is true on the other side of the house. The wife began to receive money from her husband, attention, a home, and a car. But the day came when she was thinking about all these things and forgetting about the man who provided them for her. Do you see how the situation in a home like that is deteriorating? Not because there's anything wrong with the wife doing the cooking, or with the husband bringing home money and doing things for the wife. But those things in themselves will never make a marriage. And just the way you find it with a man and his wife, so you can find it with a soul and the Lord.

All of this is brought out in the experience of Israel back in Old Testament days. In Judges 2 we read this record: "And also all that generation were gathered unto their fathers: and there arose another generation after them, which knew not the Lord, nor yet the works which he had done for Israel. And the children of Israel did evil in the sight of the Lord, and served Baalim: and they forsook the Lord God of their fathers, which brought them out of the land of Egypt, and followed other gods, of the gods of the people that were round about them, and bowed themselves unto them, and provoked the Lord to anger. And they forsook the Lord, and served Baal and Ashtaroth. And the anger of the Lord was hot against Israel" (Judges 2:10-14).

Baal and Ashtaroth are very common names in the Bible. Baal refers to the forces of nature—to nature worship, if you please. Ashtaroth was the goddess of favor and brings attention to natural pleasure. So the two symbolize the worship of natural forces and natural pleasures. A question might arise in our day and time whether or not that kind of idolatry could be. Well, where it speaks of serving Baal, suppose I put the word "science," and where you have the word Ashtaroth, suppose I put in the word "amusement." Aren't these two things people are very much taken up with today? It's interesting to note the extent to which these interests affect a person.

Do you think there's any chance today that people who belong to God could get so interested in the natural forces that we develop in science as to turn aside from God? And then, with the pleasures we have today in amusements and sports, do you think there's any chance that those things could interfere with your relationship with God? You can notice the extent of these interests if you observe the time people give to them, and the money or the energy they willingly spend. The children of Israel turned away from the things of the Lord because they became enamored with the natural forces of Baal and the natural pleasures of Ashtaroth. And today we have people who believe in the Lord Jesus Christ, but the way they live their daily life shows a greater love for science and a great interest in amusement. You can tell this by the way they spend their money and the way they occupy themselves. There will always be a substantial number who are "lovers of pleasure more than lovers of God."

People like that want all the blessings that come from Him, yet they really don't want God because they have other things in mind. It is well to bear in mind that even the people of God can foolishly turn away from Him —and we should pray we will not be in that number.

Could you believe that some religious worship is altogether displeasing to God? In Isaiah 1:15 we read a very stern word from God to the people of Israel: "And when ye spread forth your hands, I will hide mine eyes from you: yea, when ye make many prayers, I will not hear: your hands are full of blood." This word from God tells us that it is possible for people to actually go into a prayer exercise without getting God to listen. These are more souls in prison. They belong to God, but they're not free.

Insincere Worship

In this book, our study is showing us that God's people at times can do foolishly. That's a very sobering thought to me, because by the grace of God I count myself as one of His people, and I want to be found worthy among His people. And here I see in the Bible the plain truth that I could do a very foolish thing that involves my relation to God. If I allow anything to interfere with my honest attitude toward God when I'm worshipping, I'm hurting myself and everything that has value to me.

The life of God's people springs out of their faith in Him, but faith in God is not automatic. You just don't wake up in the morning, press a button and have faith. Nobody can just make up his mind and say, "Well, I'm going to believe God." I'll ask you who is God? And how are you going to believe Him? It takes more than just announcing your intentions. "Faith cometh by hearing, and hearing by the Word of God."

God's people can forsake God even while they are coming before Him in worship. Their minds can be wandering, and they can be somewhere else, even though they're physically in church or going through the exercises of prayer. Even though they're singing praises or listening to the preaching of God's Word, their minds can be somewhere else interested in the "fringe benefits" of Christianity. Interest in the "fringe benefits" of the Gospel can result in insincere worship. Going to church to worship God is a normal and healthy procedure, but you can go to church and *not* worship God. Just going to church and having your body present doesn't mean that you're worshipping God. You could go to church to meet somebody, or because somebody took you. You could go to church and be thinking about the ballgame you saw yesterday, or about the business you're going to do next week. Going to church is good, but it also sets up a situation in which you could be found insincere. If you don't really mean it, your face isn't turned to God.

Now you can also read the Bible merely as a matter of duty. You might resolve, "Well, I'm going to read the Bible every day," so you read a verse every day, and you call that Bible reading. That kind of contact with the Word of God really doesn't have much value. You need to read and study so that you actually understand God's Word; you need to try and hear what God has to say to you. Or take the matter of offering prayer. Prayer is of the very life of the Christian, but you could offer prayer as a matter of form. Why there are thousands upon thousands of Christian people who go to church and take part in the service, but as far as they're concerned, prayers are offered in a foreign language—or a dead language. Nobody in the congregation knows a single word that's being said, and what's more, to lots of them it doesn't matter. Well now, would you think God is taken in by that kind of worship?

And what about giving? I know that giving to the Lord's work is a very proper thing, and it can be associated with spiritual experience. But some people could give for show, or as a matter of prestige, or to salve their own conscience. The man who gives for those reasons might fool himself, but he certainly wouldn't fool God. And then again there is the matter of witnessing. Any number of people think that if they talk about the Bible or about religion, then they're witnessing. No, the witnessing that counts is witnessing about Jesus Christ. If you really believe that Jesus is alive, you will witness. The Scriptures say, "This people draw near me with their mouth, and with their lips do honor me, but have removed their heart far from me." People can get into the habit of religion and the habit of worship, and even while doing these things, in their hearts depart from the living God. Because God is invisible and our attitude toward Him is invisible, make-believe is so simple. I know we're not supposed to judge people, but believe me, God will judge them—and God isn't taken in by outward form.

Too many of our religious customs are insincere. People come to church, go through the ritual, sing at a certain time, and pray at a certain time. They stand at certain times and sing at certain times. And in some churches they even kneel at certain times. Now all of this can become very formal and superficial. The pastor can actually deliver a bit of a sermon disguised as a prayer. Or take church music. We sing the most profound truths in our great anthems. But I wonder how many choir members would pass an examination asking what those words mean. Some might as well be singing in a foreign language.

Years ago, when I was a young man, I had a good friend who was not a believer but had a wonderful voice, so he sang in the choir. I'll never forget the day I heard him singing, "I heard the voice of Jesus say, Come unto me and rest. Lay down thy weary one, lay down thy head upon my breast." I had to think to myself, "You sing well, but you're a liar. You did not hear the voice of Jesus." But it fooled my friend. He thought he was in a worship service, but it was all just words, and he never became a believer. Well that kind of thing is involved when God's people actually turn away from Him. their faith is going to be weak and their souls are going to be starved.

Do you think if a man were a real prophet of God everyone would listen to him, and all the believers would believe him? Prophets are preachers. Whenever you see the word "prophet" used in the Bible, you can think of a person who preaches the Word of God. Now you may imagine that prophecy has to do only with the future. Well, prophecy deals with the past, the present, and the future. In each case, it tells forth the

Rejecting the Prophet

mind of God. There are three classes of servants moving among God's people—prophets, priests and kings. The prophet takes the Word from God and explains it to the people; the priest brings the people in their need to God, and the "king" coordinates, controls, supervises among the people. But right now we're thinking about the prophet and his relationship with the people of God. In Old Testament times, His people were worshipping the forces of nature and sharing in the pleasures of nature. They'd participate in the worship of God and go through the motions, but their hearts were far away from God. Instead of exposing them for the insincere hypocrites that they were, God sent them prophets—messengers with the message of God. In our day and time these would be called revival preachers. Their basic theme was, "Thus saith the Lord." These were men who came representing God, reminding believing people of the things that God had said. In our own day there are preachers who stand up before everybody and tell them what the Word of God actually means to them. We sometimes speak of them as mass evangelists because they get a large number of people together preaching to them at the same time. But most of the evangelists of today are actually prophetic in their preaching. They are actually declaring to the whole wide world and the church in particular what the Word of God really means. They remind the people of God, "The promises of God that you have heard and that you claim to believe are actually valid and true. The Word of God is real. God's law is eternal. You're really going to have to meet with God and God is really going to deal with you according to His revealed Word."

These evangelists, wherever you hear them, are sure to be talking about sin not because they like it but because this is the disease they have come to treat. They tell the people God will not condone sin; He'll judge it and condemn it. But if they know the Gospel, they will also preach that sacrifice can be offered for sin—that there is a "Lamb of God which taketh away the sin of the world." But they will also preach to you that repentance is absolutely necessary. Many people today seem to lay claim to all the promises of God, but they never talk about repentance. That's not Biblical. Your sin will condemn you before God until you confess it and put it upon Jesus Christ

But sadly, tragically, preaching like that can be rejected—or criticized—and often is. There's never been a time when a man declared the Word of God that there were not others who got up and said, "It's not like he said." It was that way in the day of Jeremiah. It was that way in the time of Ezekiel and Isaiah. In every single case where there was a prophet of God who told the truth, there were always those around who said, "It's not like he says. It's not going to be like that." In our own day, there are men who would never be heard if they were not criticizing the great evangelists.

In my own lifetime I have seen the Bible, as the Sword of the Spirit, actually twisted out of the hand of the church. When I first became a Christian, a man who believed the Bible could stand before the public and preach it, and you could feel that what he said was indeed the Word of God. But today, the Bible has been so criticized and bypassed that it's a question in the minds of many people whether or not you can trust the Bible. And this has been especially true in the field of education, where there has been a constant resistance to the Bible. Biblical criticism has done so much to weaken the impact of the Word of God, and lately there has been a more subtle form of opposition I'd call "Biblical evasion." Even when men have the Bible, even when they read it in the pulpit, some only quote the Bible when it agrees with them. All of this is a form of rejecting prophets—and the Word of God. When the people of God do this, we shouldn't be surprised at all that faith is languishing. I'm afraid you will find in the church very little genuine faith. So many church members are not sure about heaven, not sure about sin, not sure about hell or Satan. You often wonder what they do believe.

Would you agree that there are people who are actually worshipping idols which they have made rather than the God in whom they profess to believe? "Little children, keep yourselves from idols." These are the words that are spoken by John in the last sentence of his first Epistle.

Our whole discussion in these chapters has been dealing with the Christian life. I think it's important that you keep in mind that our concern has been

Idol Worship

about the people of God. Of course, it is possible that you are reading this book but really are not a believer in the Lord Jesus Christ. If so, I hope you will find this discussion informative and helpful and perhaps even challenging. I hope that as you read these things about the Gospel of the Lord Jesus Christ, there may grow in your mind an appreciation of the reasonableness and of the sensibleness of the arrangements made by God through the Lord Jesus Christ for the salvation of His people. This whole matter of salvation as the work of God is a reasonable affair.

God made the world, and we find that natural processes have a reasonableness to them. There are reasonable things to expect so far as the spiritual world is concerned. If a person reads the Bible, studies it, gets to know what's in it, and commits himself in the spirit to God, you can expect that person to have faith. "Faith cometh by hearing, and hearing by the Word of God." That's reasonable. If you have a person who doesn't read the Bible, doesn't study it or think about it, then that person doesn't have faith. That's reasonable too. If you don't eat anything, you'll be weak. If you don't sow any seeds in the ground, you won't get a crop. And if a person doesn't read the Bible, and doesn't pray, and doesn't think about God and turn to Him, he winds up with no faith. On the other hand, if you do study the Bible, and think on these things, and yield yourself to Him, you'll have faith.

It is possible for a person, even though he believes in God, to allow things to happen that will take away his blessing. God sets him free, but he can lose his liberty. God will cleanse him, but he can become unclean. God will forgive him, but he can fall into sin, and this is what happens when certain conditions are allowed to exist.

Everything that we need in order to learn this truth was actually pictured in Israel's history. Although they were the people of God, it was possible for them to act in such a way that they fell back into bondage—and this actually did happen. For four hundred years they lived in the land of Egypt, where they became slaves. Then by the power of God, through the ministry of Moses, they were led out in the great Exodus movement, when they were delivered from the land of Egypt and brought into the land of Canaan. They were given victory over the Canaanites, and they were established as the ruling power in the land of Canaan. But through foolishness on their part, they lost their liberty and actually became the servants of the Canaanites. This was a condition that did not need to be, but it was, and it's important to recognize that Christians can lose their power too.

You can be a believer in the Lord Jesus Christ, and actually belong to God, and yet be without blessing. Israel passed through a period of time when this occurred because something was wrong in their thinking——and it had a lot to do with their worship.

When you speak of worship, you have to consider whom one worships and how one worships. Remember that worship is an act on our part where we esteem, admire, and serve, and the One we prefer in this way is God. But there are gods, many of them, that man has made that are spelled with a little "g." When someone esteems anything above God, that person or that thing becomes an idol. It's easy to tell that a man makes his own gods when they're wood and stone. It's not so easy to see this truth when man is worshipping another person, or when he worships his possessions, or when he worships his pleasures. Usually worship is a willing adoration, but sometimes worship can be in the form of fear. The man who fears would be surprised if you told him he is worshipping the things he dreads, but that's what he's doing. He's so much impressed by these evil things he can't think of anything else. Who, then, can I say is my God or my idol? It is the person who is the most important to me, or the one thing I would most freely devote my money to.

When John said, "Little children, keep yourselves from idols," he was referring to this tendency to let the attention of the heart become focused upon something other than God. Remember the Scriptural exhortation spoken to all mankind, "Thou shalt worship the Lord thy God and Him only shalt thou serve." We're to put

God first. Something or someone other than God is a
form of idol worship. Some men make an idol of business, or the "almighty dollar." You may say, "Oh they
don't really think money is god." But wait, where will
they invest their time? What will they put first? Here is a
time when the people are going to worship God, but a
man says, "Well, business calls—I've got to go." He is
making business—profit—his god. Some people
wouldn't go to a prayer meeting because they belong to a
certain family, and that family has never gone to a prayer
meeting, and they don't want to have a bad name in that
family. Some people never go to a revival service because they want to have a good standing with people
who are against revival. There are people who have
positions they think of more than they think about God.
There are people who will take time out for pleasure but
wouldn't take time out to go to church. There are people
who will spend more money on sports or amusements
than they would put in the offering at church. There are
some people to whom science is far more important than
God. In the field of education, there are people far more
impressed with the library than they are with the Bible.
And all of these things are ways in which a person can
actually allow other things to come in and take the first
place ahead of God. "Thou shalt worship the Lord thy
God and him only shalt thou serve." God is to come first
in our lives.

The
Judgment
of God

Do you realize that when active opposition and hostility develop against a believer, this may be the judgment of God upon him? "And the anger of the Lord was hot against Israel, and he delivered them into the hands of spoilers that spoiled them, and he sold them into the hands of their enemies round about, so that they could not any longer stand before their enemies" (Judges 2:14). When a person who belongs to God foolishly forsakes Him, like a child straying away from its mother, it is of the mercy and the grace of God that he is not cut at once. Actually God will work to turn him back. In this chapter, I'd like to consider some of the ways in which God would act to bring a foolish person to his senses. Here is a person who really believes in God, but he never reads the Bible, stops going to church, and never prays. What's going to happen to that foolish man? God will work with him, because God cares about him.

Raising Up Enemies

The text at the beginning of this chapter says that though Israel was His people, "the anger of the Lord was hot against Israel," He let them fall into the hands of godless people who robbed them and spoiled them. In order to bring His people to their senses, God actually let them get into some hard trouble and have some awful experiences. He sold them into the hands of their enemies. And now we're going to consider how God, in seeking to awaken His people and turn them from their foolish ways, may raise up hostile opposition that will bring His people to the sense of their need.

I'm not talking about personal enemies. We all have those, because we have rivals—competitors. I'm not even talking about "family feud" kind of enmity. I'm talking about spiritual enemies—people or influences that are against the interests of a Christian. Now exactly what are a Christian's interests? Wouldn't you agree with me that every person who is a Christian wants the welfare and fortune of his loved ones? He wants his loved ones to be protected from harm and to have faith in God, and he wants good will in the family. A Christian also wants faithfulness in fellow-believers. wouldn't you like to be in a church where everybody else was a true believer? Wouldn't you like to be in a company of believers who were all acting like real Christians? Well, spiritual enemies would fight against all that. And so the Christian would find that subversive elements were active against him.

Here's a person trying to bring up his children in the ways of God but he, himself, is neglecting God. He doesn't have Bible reading in his home, and he doesn't take the children to Sunday School regularly, and he doesn't pray. So what happens? Suddenly he finds that his children have doubts about God, doubts about the Bible. And right in his family, right in his church, there is a tolerance of evil and scoffing of those who are good. Unbelief will grow, and open sin will take place. The enemy is moving in; he's being robbed. His children had some faith at first, but they lost it. By the time they've gotten through high school and into college, they don't have it anymore. They've been robbed too.

In this study, we've seen that so far as the people of God are concerned, they can be guilty of foolish neglect; they can forsake God as they turn their hearts and minds to other things. They can fall into formality and insincerity in their religious life. And when a faithful revival preacher comes along, they can reject him or ignore him. And in so doing, God's people can actually offend God. It is human to err, I know, but there is no way under heaven to explain why a hungry person won't eat, or a thirsty person won't drink. But that's what God's people are doing when they commit their hearts to things other than God. And now we are to see that when God's people do that, God brings judgment.

Look at Judges 4:1-2 where it says, "And the children of Israel again did evil in the sight of the Lord . . . And the Lord sold them into the hand of Jabin king of Canaan." Or look on a little further: "The children of Israel did evil in the sight of the Lord: and the Lord delivered them into the hand of Midian seven years." Then again: "And the anger of the Lord was hot against Israel, and he sold them into the hands of the Philistines." They were the people of God, but they had turned away from God and angered Him. And now He's chastening them. The only way to wake them up is to let them suffer the consequences of their conduct. God lets troubles come in.

It's always true when a man's ways please the Lord, He makes even his enemies to be at peace with him. But our study is showing us the way God deals with His people when they foolishly turn away from Him and neglect Him. In the text, we saw that He raises up enemies that will rob them. We see this over and over again in the case of people who really believe in God, but have chosen something that is second best. Their homes aren't blessed; their children aren't blessed; their churches aren't blessed; their business isn't blessed. They belong to God, but they are souls in prison. Thank God, though, He can deliver them. Before we are through with our study, we're going to see how He does it in Christ Jesus.

Does it surprise you that in spite of all their defeats, the people of God expect to win the victory? After all, a Christian is a human being who is letting God have His way in his soul—a person who is yielding himself into the hands of God that he might obey the will of the Lord Jesus Christ. Salvation is what happens when Christ Jesus works in the human heart and activates in the believer to do the will of Almighty God.

Defeat in Battle

But we've found that people who really do belong to God and have yielded themselves to Him can actually be found forsaking the Lord. They can become enamored again with the things of the world. In this world we're ambassadors, and we live in this world as those who are citizens of another world. But as a Christian lives in this world, he faces many things that contradict his best interests spiritually. Sometimes these overwhelm him. Yet such has been the experience of God's people that we can be confident that if a person is obedient to God he can expect victory. He can expect to be on the winning side. Look at this promise in Joshua 1:5: "There shall not any man be able to stand before thee all the days of thy life: as I was with Moses, so I will be with thee: I will not fail thee, nor forsake thee." That's a strong promise, but a stipulation follows: "Only be thou strong and very courageous, that thou mayest observe to do according to all the law." God places a lot of importance on man doing what His Word says. "This book of the law shall not depart out of thy mouth; but thou shalt meditate therein day and night, that thou mayest observe to do according to all that is written therein: for then thou shalt make thy way prosperous, and then thou shalt have good success." That promise was given to God's people telling them He would be with them. And yet these same people suffered defeat as you read in Joshua 7:7-8. "And Joshua said, Alas, O Lord God, wherefore hast thou at all brought this people over Jordan, to deliver us into the hand of the Amorites, to destroy us? would to God we had been content, and dwelt on the other side Jordan! O Lord, what shall I say, when Israel turneth their backs before their enemies!" They had been defeated, and this shook Joshua badly—left him prostrate. If God should let His people go down in defeat, they might well be utterly destroyed. But verse 10 says, "And the Lord said unto Joshua, Get thee up; wherefore liest thou thus upon thy face? Israel hath sinned, and they have also transgressed my covenant which I commanded them." In verses 12 and 13, He states the case very bluntly: "Therefore the children of Israel could not stand before their enemies, but turned their backs before their enemies, because they were accursed: neither will I be with you any more, except ye destroy the accursed from among you. Up, sanctify the people, and say, Sanctify yourselves against tomorrow: for thus saith the Lord God of Israel, There is an accursed thing in the midst of thee, O Israel: thou canst not stand before thine enemies, until ye take away the accursed thing from among you." This happened again and again in the history of Israel, until finally God was moved to enact devastating judgment against them.

The only possible way Israel could win any of its battles was by the help of the Lord. There were never enough of them, and they were never strong enough——but with God they were invincible. Yet God would walk with them only if they were obedient. And let me show you how Christians are being defeated in the spiritual battles they wage in this very day and time because of disobedience. Consider the home life of many Christians. How often do you find there is no daily Bible reading, no daily prayer, no real reverence toward God? They send their children to Sunday School, but too often feel no need of attending themselves. And all the time they expect something good from God. How many people do you know who make their profession of faith, get their names on the church rolls, and claim all the benefits of Christianity, but don't come to the worship services and never talk to other people about the Lord? They don't sow any seed, but they want a crop. And what do you find among them as a result? All too often, you find them in doubt, unbelief, and sin. That's defeat, and that kind of defeat comes naturally with disobedience. In fact, they *should* be defeated when they care no more than that about victory.

When you find Christians without any interest in evangelism, no interest in seeking to win other people to Christ, no interest in getting to know what the Bible actually says, you will also find doubt, unbelief, and sin. And that's nothing but defeat. They really and truly wanted to be strong in the Lord, but they turned out to be weaklings. God's people can go down in defeat for no other reason than that they forsook God and neglected the things of the Lord.

Do you think much was lost when the churches gave up the mid-week prayer meeting? God's people get a great many advantages from fellowship together. It is true that the individual turns to God, and God saves the individual, but then that individual finds he shares life with a group. And the individual in sharing life with other people enters into fulfillment of his own life. It's not good for a man to be alone. But you can't

Destruction of Jerusalem

work as a mob either. You have to be organized and set out in patterns with some semblance of order. You should have leaders, and then subleaders—people who are qualified to guide the others.

You see this organization and leadership at every level of society. When a man says he lives at 755 Hill Street, you know that Hill Street is a place in a city, and 755 is a place on Hill Street. You know that he has banded together with other human beings in a community, with elected leaders and laws. His city has houses and streets and sidewalks and bridges. It has street lights and water fountains, shopping centers and fireplugs. And spiritual life is the same way. A certain structure and organization is necessary.

When God's people came together, they built a city and called it Jerusalem, the city of God. The people built and worked together in order that they might worship God together. They built their own Temple, yet Israel because of her foolishness, disobedience, and carelessness came under God's judgment. Part of that judgment was the destruction of Jerusalem—the whole city was torn up and devastated.

The same kind of destruction goes on in the spiritual lives of people all around us. Let me see if I can put it to you this way: the church is a group of people banding together for the purpose of worshipping God. The individual Christian comes into that church and is accepted by his brethren as one of the group. The church will usually have a Sunday School where the Word of God is taught and a place where the young people come together in fellowship. In the church services they sing praises to God—hymns that have been written by people—and they learn to sing them together. Still, it is many individuals who do the singing. The church has seasons of congregational prayer, but it is an individual person who is actually praying. Then they may all join in the Lord's Prayer, or in reciting the Apostles' Creed. They have other customs and practices that involve organization and instruction—like baptism for example. There's a prescribed way to perform the ceremony as a witness to the world outside.

Many congregations have some way of challenging the individual to openly confess his Savior. There are certain questions to ask, and certain answers to be expected. Most churches have some sort of plan for visitation and group witnessing. The people join together to help the poor, and you share in that if you're a part of the church. In addition, the church will have Bible study at certain times. There are prayer meetings at the church and cottage prayer meetings and special prayer meetings. Each congregation has its own patterns. It has a certain way of going about marriage and has a pre-scribed funeral service. The church speaks of the Bible as the Word of God. It thinks reading and studying the Bible helps us to understand what God wants, so the church has a certain attitude toward that. It has doc-trines that have been spelled out—like the matter of being born again, or the doctrine of the Holy Spirit, or Heaven and Hell.

Now I've quickly run over a great many things that are structured. These are customs and practices that are important to every Christian. But I want you to see how easily all of this can be jeopardized. Christians could lose everything that I've talked about. How? By neg-lect—by not going to church or Sunday School, not lis-tening to the Word of God, not singing or praying, paying no attention to baptism. Just don't get up to confess Christ, never bring anybody to church, don't do anything for the poor and this will be your dilemma.

We have in the church today people who criticize the Bible on the basis of what is called scholarship. They say you can't take it word for word. Christian experience is criticized from the point of view of psychology. One person will tell what happened to him when he became a Christian, and someone with psychological training will reinterpret all of that to show that nothing really hap-pened to him. The church program is criticized as failing in some aspect of sociology. If you criticize the things of God this way you can jeopardize and destroy every blessing of which I have spoken.

When Israel got to a certain point on its downhill course, God let Babylon come in and destroy the city of

Jerusalem. That was the city of the people of God. They had neglected God, lost their own testimony, and the time came when God left them, and they lost everything. If the city of Jerusalem could be destroyed, then Christian character can be destroyed. We are dependent upon the mercy of God, yet God will save us if we put our trust in Him and humbly commit ourselves to Him.

Can you understand the importance of a Christian having confidence in what he is doing when he worships God? We are studying the living experiences of a Christian, and worship is one of the most important of them all. Now it may be that you have never come to a definite personal relationship with God, not yet reached the point of a definite commitment to God. If you want the spiritual blessing that God has made possible in Christ Jesus, you must be born again.

Destruction of the Temple

But on the other hand you may count yourself a Christian. You have put your confidence in Jesus Christ, and you're coming to God through Him. Well, it is for you especially that I am preparing these chapters. We're discussing the living experiences of a Christian, and we're pointing out that a Christian person can actually lose the benefits of the very Gospel in which he believes. You can be a Christian and not get anything out of it because of an unhappy relationship with God. But just now I want you to see that the experiences of a Christian occur in his consciousness, and in his consciousness the language that he is aware of, the words in which he thinks, are very important. Much of the conscious experience of a Christian involves language. There are words and symbols and procedures which the Christian uses when he comes to worship God. The worship of God employs certain language and certain symbols. Often the Christian carries on his worship in a place which he calls a sanctuary. Originally there was an altar, a place where the worshipper brought his sacrifice and made his prayers and where God would meet with him. The altar was in the sanctuary. In time, the sanctuary together with other rooms was in a building spoken of as the Temple. Now all of these things—altars, sanctuaries, temples—are related to the Christian experience of worshipping. In worship, a person must think, and for thinking you need words. Now since God is invisible, it is necessary that the truth of God be supernaturally revealed, and this revelation must come in words so that man can see or hear them.

The Christian uses certain means in his worship, and all of these means he has received from others. A Christian uses the Bible, but he didn't write the Bible—he didn't even translate it. From the Scripture we get certain doctrines. A Christian person coming before God has certain ideas about God and about God's ways that have been taught to him in his doctrine. There are certain procedures that he will follow. There are the sacraments of baptism and the Lord's Supper. There is the profession of faith—the preaching of the Word. There is the ordaining of church officers. All of these things are a part of worship, and the Christian knowing about these things carries them out with confidence in God. All of these things are largely inherited from pioneers who developed them as being useful in the worship of God. Now the intelligent and diligent use of means is effectual. When a Christian reads the Bible, remembers the doctrine and practices the ritual, understands the theology and exercises himself in witnessing—that Christian person is going to grow. There's no question about it.

The diligent use of such intelligent means is effectual. Any Christian is fortunate when he has confidence in what he is doing. But just now I want to bring to your attention that there are people who suffer loss through neglect of God, and they lose their confidence in these very things.

When the people of God let their devotion languish so that they no longer seek God's face, the judgment of God is to be seen in the loss of their confidence in the means of worship. Now all of this was demonstrated in the destruction of Jerusalem, because at the time Jerusalem was destroyed the enemy also destroyed the Temple. Here is the record in 2 Kings 25:13-15: "And the pillars of brass that were in the house of the Lord, and the bases, and the brasen sea that was in the house of the Lord, did the Chaldees break in pieces, and carried the brass of them to Babylon." They stripped the Temple of all its brass. "And the pots, and the shovels, and the snuffers, and the spoons, and all the vessels of brass wherewith they ministered, took they away." They took all the brass home. "And the firepans, and the bowls, and such things as were of gold, in gold, and of silver, in silver, the captain of the guard took away." In the destruction of Jerusalem and in the capture by Nebuchadnezzar the whole city and the Temple were despoiled.

When we bring that over to our own day, you may ask how I apply it to us. How will I understand that as a Christian, because I don't worship in a Temple like that. In what way could a Christian lose his means of worship? Well let me go over the things I mentioned to you. The Christian uses the Bible in his worship. In our day, with the neglect by the church of the actual meaning of the Bible, the Bible has been left in the hands of critics, of people who don't believe it. Today throughout the church the Bible is questioned. There are many people who believe in the Lord Jesus Christ but who have lost their confidence in the Bible. There was nothing in the Bible that made them lose their confidence, but things have been said about it that cause the Bible to be questioned. Take the doctrines the Christian church has traditionally held—like "the soul that sinneth it shall die," and that only those who come to God through the Lord Jesus Christ will be saved. People don't want to believe that today. These doctrines are doubted throughout the church.

When a wedding ceremony is held in the church and the pastor hears the marriage vows, how many people today really intend to keep those vows? Or take the matter of the Lord's Supper. It's provided in the Scriptures for people who believe in the Lord Jesus Christ, but do you suppose everybody is trusting in the Lord Jesus Christ who partakes of the Lord's Supper? When you hear a singer today in church, how often can you believe he means exactly what he is singing? There was a time when if Christians didn't mean it they wouldn't say it. Do you think today when church people go out witnessing and asking others to come to church they really have in mind the salvation of that soul? The fact is, our means of worship, our attitude toward the Bible, our doctrines, our practices, our theology, our witnessing—these things are subject to deterioration, and we suffer because of this. In other chapters, we're going to see how badly we suffer.

Do you realize how much of our worship in the Christian church is actually controlled by others? Our interest in our present studies is in the people of God and their experiences. We want to learn about them because we want to understand ourselves. I want to show you from the Old Testament and from the experiences of Israel that God's people can actually get into a condition where they are really losing the very blessings

Taken Captive

and benefits promised them in the Gospel. You see, living as a Christian is not a simple matter. A person can be fooled, and he can make mistakes.

It's a common thing for people to think that the Christian church is largely for "weaklings," and there is a sense in which you can understand why the public doesn't know any better. It's a very common thing to see guilty people turning to God—so you quickly conclude that everybody who turns to God is guilty. Weak people call upon God, and you feel that everybody who prays is weak. Bewildered people seek the face of God, and so you get the notion that anyone who wants to know the Lord is bewildered. The impression grows that the Christian Gospel is for the guilty, the weak, and the bewildered. And sometimes Christians themselves fall into this way of thinking, and so they're inclined to yield too much control over to other people. Now, it's true that the Bible makes a virtue out of yielding to the Lord. But there are those who tell you that if you're a real Christian you shouldn't stand up for anything, you should just give in on every side. The problem comes when parts of our church life—our Christian experience—is controlled by people who are not Christian. This fact can cause us tragic loss. Certain definite achievements that came out of the history of the church can be lost by our present generation. Protestant Reformers risked their lives to get the Bible open and into the hands of the people. But Protestants today can actually have the Bible taken away from them through clever dealing with the Scripture by people who are not Christians themselves.

You can lose the blessings of the Gospel, even though you're a child of God. You can lose them through neglecting them. In 2 Kings 24:10, we read where enemies came in and took over everything that the people of God had. Because of their incorrigible wayward-ness, their disobedience, their unwillingness to go by the way of God, the Israelites suffered a complete loss of the things that they had. "At that time the servants of Nebuchadnezzar king of Babylon came up against Jeru-salem, and the city was besieged. And Nebuchadnezzar king of Babylon came against the city, and his servants did besiege it." Israel's King Jehoiachin yielded to him, and then in verse 13 we read, "And he carried out thence all the treasures of the house of the Lord and the treas-ures of the king's house, and cut in pieces all the vessels of gold which Solomon king of Israel had made in the temple of the Lord, as the Lord had said." So you see, Jehoiachin the king of Judah yielded to Nebuchadnezzer and all the gold vessels were carried out and cut up in pieces and taken away by the king. But more than that, "And he carried away all Jerusalem, and all the princes, and all the mighty men of valor, even ten thousand captives, and all the craftsmen and smiths: none remained, save the poorest sort of the people of the land." By the help of God His people could and they did have victory over their enemies, but in neglecting the thing of God and forsaking Him, they provoked God so that He withdrew His favor. History records that the pagans came and captured and despoiled the city and carried the people away as captives.

Today pagan forces do not carry the people of God away in a physical sense to some geographical location. They don't take us out of one part of the country and take us over into another part of the country, but they completely dominate the people of God in a psychological and cultural way. By skillful brainwashing, Christians have been robbed of their confidence, and strength, and they have been ensnared. Take for instance the matter of calling a pastor. What are the traits they look for in a minister of the Gospel? How seldom do you find that what they want in the pastor is a spiritually minded man. More often, they want a man who is a good mixer. What do they mean by that? Someone the public will like. They want to be sure the man will be able to increase the number of the church and make it a success. They don't ask how it is between himself and the Lord, because that's not the particular thing they have in mind. You could guess that by taking a look at their program for the week—examining all the activities that are going on within the congregation.

Look at the church bulletin and ask where the praying is being done. Where are the meetings actually scheduled for praying and for Bible study? Who has influenced the church to give all its attention to other activities?

When someone joins the church today, instead of actual examination to find out whether that person really believes in the Lord and understands the Gospel, we generally find the questions are very informal and his answers are vague, and then he's voted in. Then we wonder why the church isn't strong. Why should it be strong? To what extent do we think we are actually partaking of the Lord's Supper when we don't search our hearts, come worthily, remembering Him and His death until He comes? And what about the way we use our Bibles today? People don't any longer have confidence in it. How often can you listen to preachers preach or Sunday School teachers teach without hearing the word "saved," or the word "hell?" This is what happens when the people have been taken captive. They're not master of their own minds.

I am desperately trying to awaken members of the church, believers in the Lord Jesus Christ, to the danger that comes through neglect. You could lose your blessings, and you'll find that your heart and mind are taken over by other ideas that are not true to the Gospel of the Lord Jesus Christ.

In Captivity

Can you see the importance of a man having a definite procedure to follow when he comes to worship God? In these studies we're learning what happens to God's people when through neglect a believer becomes imprisoned in his own ignorance and unbelief. Christian people have a great advantage over others. They already know that Jesus of Nazareth is the Son of God, and they know that He died for them, and they know that they have been accepted by God in Christ Jesus. They are then what we would call the people of God. But the people of God can get into a condition where, through their own personal neglect, they become ignorant of what they should know, and they fail to believe the things they're committed to. They actually come into spiritual bondage.

No Temple

By studying the history of the Israelites, who lived in this world for a length of time as the people of God, we can learn much about experiences that the people of God have today. In His guidance of His people, way back in the days of Moses, God revealed the pattern of the Tabernacle. This was a structured condition of mind for acceptable worship. If a person came into the presence of God, there were certain things he should have in mind when he came. Just anybody cannot come to God any way he pleases. Thank God, anybody can come to God at any time in humility and in penitence, asking for mercy, and God will hear his cry. But if that person wants to walk with God, if he wants to have communion with God, there are things he needs to know. God revealed through Moses a certain ritual of procedure which if followed, would bring the heart of the worshipper into full communion with God. And this was set forth first in the Tabernacle and afterwards in the Temple, and provided as an authorized structure of conditions under which any sinner could come into the presence of God. This enabled the worshipper to come appropriately by reminding him of the things that he really believed. It kept him from neglect, from just going through the motions. In judgment upon the people of God, God allowed pagans, complete unbelievers to come in and to destroy the Temple. Today in the time we are living, there are certain standard elements in true worship that any Christian person would recognize. I want to mention to you very soberly that through neglect, through indifference, through unbelief, the whole procedure of worship may become so formal and so empty that it is totally unacceptable to God. God in judgment may allow pagans, people that don't believe in Him at all, to actually destroy traditional elements.

Let me point out what some of those elements are. In coming to the God of the Bible, the worshipper should first of all come with repentance. There isn't any way to come to God that doesn't begin with repentance. Now if there is repentance of heart there is confession of sin with the mouth. This is reflected in the routine questions to an applicant for membership which draw attention to that person's sin and that person's confession of sin. In the very hymns that we sing, repentance is taught. "At the cross, at the cross, where I first saw the light, and the burden of my heart rolled away." All of this is basic in Christian experience and through neglecting it, taking it for granted, God has allowed pagans, unbelievers, to come at the whole matter of repentance from a psychological approach. They've attacked what they call "the guilt complex" until you have many people who call themselves Christians who have no consciousness of sin. Another important element of the Christian experience is submission. When a Christian comes to God, it's natural for him to surrender to God. And this involves a repudiation of worldliness. This repudiation of worldliness will show up in his habits; it will show up in where he goes and in what he does.

I can remember so well years ago, before I was a Christian, at a service one evening in Canada, where an earnest plea had been made for people to give themselves to God, and two young men went forward. When they came out of that church building, one took a packet of cigarettes out of his pocket and threw them out into the woods. He said, "Well, there goes that!" And I can remember thinking how that's the way it would be if a person became a Christian—some things you'd just "lop" off. But we've neglected that. We don't raise any question about conduct anymore. And you know what has happened? Pagans have attacked what they sneeringly refer to as "piety." They've made it a bad word, and the way they've talked about it has resulted in the destruction of the Temple—just like in the old days. Now there is no self-denial, no consciousness of sin.

A few years ago, if a person accepted Jesus Christ as

Savior, you would expect him to begin to follow the Lord, and that would mean there would be Bible study. He would normally indicate an interest in what the Bible teaches. But now we've gotten to where a person can be recognized as a Christian all his life but never know the basic truths taught in the Bible. What has happened? Pagans have attacked the Bible. They've attacked the whole concept of revelation. How in the world can the church expect to retain faith when it doesn't study the Bible? It's just as though the Temple had been destroyed.

It's normal for a Christian person to give thanks. Christians would normally be expected to give thanks to God for blessings received. You expect them to practice praying and praising God. But Christians have neglected prayer and neglected praise, and pagans have moved in and attacked the whole idea of worship as being impractical.

It's been a common thing through the years to expect a Christian to have a personal experience of communion with the Lord—a face to face relationship. But now, from Monday morning till Saturday night, Christians pay no attention to the things of the Lord. Pagans have attacked the whole concept of holiness. They've made us feel that holiness is impractical. It's just as it was in the old days in Israel. They had a Temple, and in the Temple was the altar, the laver, the candlesticks, the table of shewbread, the altar of incense—and these things were all destroyed because they neglected them. God allowed the pagans to come in and wipe them out until they had nothing. This is what you have today, with no repentance, no consciousness of sin, no surrender to God, no self-denial, no following the Lord, no Bible study, no giving thanks, no prayer meetings, and no personal fellowship with God. And actually such Christian people—though they do believe in the Lord Jesus Christ—are like souls in prison.

Do you realize that the normal experience of a real Christian is to have victory at all times? "Now thanks be unto God, which always causeth us to triumph in Christ" (2 Corinthians 2:14). But there are many conditions contrary to blessing. This world is not favorable to spiritual life. When a person has faith, that's an achievement. You have to win to have hope. If you want to have love, you have to overcome. It's not

No Victory

a simple thing to live a Christian life. When a person says, "Well, you'll be a Christian if you just believe," that phrase, "just believe," could mislead you. It isn't quite that simple.

Faith in Jesus Christ needs to be nurtured and established. Through the years, Christians have followed Biblical patterns that developed their faith. Yet because of indifference, and because of failing to use the privileges which are theirs, these patterns can be lost. And when they are, the soul of the worshipper doesn't have a path to follow in coming to God. This is illustrated in the time in Israel's experience when the nation of Babylon came in and captured Jerusalem and destroyed the city. They destroyed the Temple. Then for some time the people of God, the children of Israel, lived in captivity. They were souls in prison. During that time, they lost everything they depended on as a guidance for the way in which they would go. They no longer had the Temple to guide them in their worship of God. They also lost certain understanding, and when they lost this spiritual discernment, they were just like someone who needed to cross a country but had no roads to travel on. This is how some people now live as Christians. They neglected what they had, and they lost it.

You and I enjoy certain privileges and benefits that were won by other people in days gone by at great cost. We can lose them, and you can lose them very easily. Let me mention some of the things Christian people can lose through neglect. You can lose your consciousness of the atoning work of Jesus Christ. You can forget that Christ Jesus in dying for us reconciled us to God and brought us into fellowship with Him. There is no sense of being at one with God. Instead, there is a consciousness of guilt. If God isn't there to forgive, there's guilt. And this results in the fear of judgment and in a bad conscience. You'd be surprised how many Christian people are afraid of the judgment of God. Many a Christian is heartsick when he thinks about dying and going into the presence of God. Confidence in the atoning work of Jesus Christ was wiped out of his memory through neglect.

When a person becomes a Christian, he feels in his heart he should yield himself to God. But he neglects that impulse and soon is ensnared in his own desires. His own interests and appetites take him captive, and he becomes a captive to his own sinful tendencies. He is a soul in prison. And something else has been lost—the consciousness of the presence of God that we commonly associate with the Holy Spirit. And because of neglect and unbelief, there's no Holy Spirit operative in the soul. If I don't have God working in me, then I'm on my own, and I'm not strong enough. If you have no consciousness of the presence of God, then you're alone, and you can't do what you should do.

I'm speaking of Christians—people who really do believe in God and really do belong to God but who neglected the practices. They neglected their relationship with God, and now they have no knowledge of the Bible. They really don't know the promises of God. And if they don't know the promises of God, then unbelief is there, and it spreads everywhere with its paralyzing effect.

A Christian is called to deny himself, take up his cross and follow the Lord Jesus Christ. And the call to deny himself is a normal Christian experience. If it's neglected, and the Christian doesn't deny himself, he'll look around and see that other Christians don't deny themselves, and just allows things to drift. And if he doesn't deny himself, there will be in him no humility, and if he's not humbling himself in the sight of God and in the sight of other men, then the result will be pride. Because this Christian forgot about self-denial, he fell into the sin of pride. This is one of the reasons there is so little victory among God's people. They belong to Him because they trust in Him. They believe in Him, but they haven't been working at it. They have a fear of judgment—a bad conscience about what they have done. They are helpless to change their ways—they are marked with unbelief. When a Christian lives this way he is unhappy, critical of others, and the victim of strange ideas. He's in bondage, and he lives in defeat. All of this is the result of neglect of the things of the Lord. Isn't it tragic to think this could happen to a Christian?

Have you ever considered how important hope is to our feelings? "Having no hope and without God in the world"—this is what the Apostle Paul used for describing the condition of people without Christ, and that truly is a sad condition for anybody. There are many circumstances in life as we face them that are unfavorable to us. All day long we battle against things that threaten to undo us. But we can go on with what

No Hope

we're doing if we can have the hope, if we can cherish the expectation of eventual victory.

To have hope, one must have some kind of ground on which he can base his confidence. In the case of a Christian who has a degree of understanding in his faith, his hope is composed of several elements. He understands, and he believes that God is benevolent. He looks around him, and he sees many evidences of the fact that the overruling hand of God is kind. Then again, another one of his conditions for optimism is that God is gracious. He'll do more for us than we deserve, and this is seen in Christ Jesus. Then again, the Christian is convinced that God is able. He can do what He promises. And God is wise. That's seen in His providence, in the way in which He arranges things. When all these things are in the mind and in the heart of a person, he can have hope for the future. Hope looks forward to some future possibility. When you say that a man has hope, it means he's looking ahead, and what he is moving toward makes everything he does meaningful. If you were to see a woman standing at a table, surrounded by oddshaped pieces of tissue paper, cutting pieces of cloth to match, it might look as if she were cutting out paper dolls. But she's actually making a wedding gown from a pattern. Instead of being a childish affair like cutting out paper dolls, this is going to produce a wedding gown. It is the end result of the wedding gown that gives meaning to everything being done. If you asked that woman what she was doing, she wouldn't say she was cutting out materials or entertaining herself—she would say she was making a wedding dress

Hope is like that wedding gown. It's the end result that you look forward to. Don't the children look forward with happiness and gladness to the coming of Christmas Day? Isn't it true in the summertime that when the children know all week long that on Saturday there's going to be a picnic, doesn't the whole week pass along a whole lot better because you're expecting Saturday? The hopeful, you see, are the gladdest, and it's true on the other hand that "hope deferred maketh the heart sick." If your hope is taken away, your joy is gone. Hopeless people are always unhappy. But of all people in the world, the Christian is the one with the most reason to have hope. When the people of God neglect the promises of God, don't read their Bible, don't worship God, don't pray, they begin to doubt. And just as sure as doubt comes in, hope dies. When the people of God have no hope, they lose their patience, and they lose their strength. Their joy is gone—the heart is empty, and the spirit becomes critical. People like that are hard to live with.

The only person who can expect a future filled with victory is the person with faith. If you have this hope, then you have blessing—but where there's no hope there's no blessing. And this is the condition of a person who has allowed himself to be robbed of his faith because of his neglect and indifference.

Can you understand that only the confident can be strong? Christian living depends entirely on faith in God. So far as Christians are concerned, their experience in life is something that is special for them. Other people wouldn't understand it. The one great thing about a Christian is that he's not alone. He has his faith, and his hope is in God. That means that day by day and all day long God is with him. Faith has specific promises that are to be believed, but this is grounded in a general confidence in God.

No Confidence

In my personal affairs, as I live a day at a time, I know that I may face possible sorrow anytime. I can look on each experience with confidence. I know everything won't be smooth—my experiences won't all be favorable—and yet I can have assurance. But confidence in God is generated, just like confidence in man. Someone may ask, "How can I get confidence in God?" Well, how would you get confidence in any man? You'll find out you have confidence in a man when you know him——when you've been around him. Now this is what happens between you and God, and this is why the usual means of grace are so important when it comes to having confidence in God. To worship God regularly begets confidence in Him. What do I mean by worshipping God regularly? I mean going to church and sharing in the public worship of God. If I go to church regularly, I hear His name being praised, and I begin to feel that He is praiseworthy. When I go to church, I hear the Scriptures read. The Scriptures will be read as if they meant what they said, and if I hear the Scriptures read that way, I get the feeling in my own being that the Scriptures are the Word of God. This is part of the confidence I need.

Church is where you'll hear the Gospel being proclaimed, and as you get to know God better through His messenger you're going to realize it's true that "God so loved the world that He gave His only begotten Son, that whosoever believeth in Him should not perish but have everlasting life." You'll get the feeling that if "God spared not His own Son, but freely gave Him up for us all, how shall He not with Him also freely give us all things?" This grounds your confidence. Now we begin to see the sad tragedy of those who believe in God, but who through neglect wound up as souls in prison. If a man is a Christian but never goes to church, he does not hear God's name praised. He will hear God's name questioned; he will hear God's name profaned, but he won't hear God's name praised. He'll forget that God is worthy. Someone may say, "But he didn't intend to forget." Well, that's a good deal like getting wet in a rainstorm. If I go out when it's raining, it doesn't matter whether or not I intend to get wet. It isn't my intentions—it's the rain that makes me wet. If I get out of touch with public worship, I'll forget that God is worthy, and I'll lose my confidence in Him.

You see, you can't trump up confidence. You can't make believe about assurance. If you believe, thank the Lord. If you don't believe, your day is a dark day, because faith is what brings light into your life. And the

Christian who doesn't go to church, doesn't read his Bible, doesn't pray, and doesn't witness for God is neglecting the means of grace. Soon he'll have no temple—no hope or confidence in God. And this man will have no strength to resist temptation. When temptation comes up, he'll stand in his own strength and he'll fall. This kind of a person will have no joy in his daily experience. And what a dissatisfied soul he will be! I'm talking about a person who believes that Christ Jesus died for him. He really and truly believes there is a Heaven, and he believes that people who believe in Christ will go there, and yet because he neglects his fellowship with God he becomes unfruitful and unhappy. This is the condition of a soul in prison.

*Yet
There is
Hope*

If you were caught in a traffic jam somewhere, wouldn't a policeman's whistle sound awfully good?

In the life of the children of Israel, we have seen that although they belonged to God, they lost their benefits. They lost the privileges they had as believers in the God of Abraham, Isaac, and Jacob. They fell into slavery and became unhappy, miserable beings. But what interests us now is how they went about getting out of that situation—for Israel did get out of it. After they had been defeated by Babylon and had spent seventy years in captivity, God's people were released.

Ezekiel, "Thus Saith the Lord"

When Ezekiel was preaching to the people by the river Chebar, they were captive Jews in a foreign land. They were miserable; they were not blessed, and Ezekiel came to preach to them. But they didn't want to listen to him. They had a feeling of cynicism about the whole business. But when God said to Ezekiel, "Go, get thee to them of the captivity, unto the children of thy people, and speak unto them, and tell them, Thus saith the Lord God; whether they will hear, or whether they will forbear."

If you should be in a traffic jam, with everybody wanting to go in his own direction and nobody getting any place because everybody's in the way of everybody else, what would you wish to hear? You would like to hear a policeman's whistle, bringing some order out of that confusion. If a fire broke out in your house and it looked like it was going to burn down, what sound would you be listening for on the street? Wouldn't it be the fire siren? In a time of confusion—in a time of distress—we need someone to come in who knows what to do and can do it. This is what is needed by the soul in prison.

When the children of Israel found themselves down in the land of Egypt, reduced to slavery and abused and persecuted by Pharaoh, what did God do? He sent Moses, a man from the outside, with a message from God. That brought about the deliverance of the children of Israel from Egypt. Later on, when through their foolishness they fell under the rule of the Midianites and lost their liberty, what voice brought them help? It was the voice of Gideon that set them free. When the Northern Nation of Israel fell under the control of Baal worshippers in the time of Ahab and Jezebel, whose voice led them out of that defeat into victory? Was it not Elijah, the Prophet of God, who challenged them saying, "If the Lord be God, follow Him." When Judah, the Southern Kingdom, fell to Babylon, they became souls in prison again. In the providence of God, Nehemiah was the one that led them out.

You find the same thing to be true in our day and time. We're interested in these things as Christians and concerned about how they apply to the people of God today who have fallen into distress. They belong to God, but they cannot rejoice in Him. What kind of voice needs to be heard? Is it not the preacher who comes to the people saying, "Thus saith the Lord God." What is it that marks revival preaching with power? It is that these preachers talk about God and what He has said. They talk about repentance, the Gospel, and the coming of the Lord Jesus Christ. They preach about Pentecost, and tell how God sent the Holy Spirit into the hearts of men. They speak about right living, and tell you that "without holiness no man should see the Lord." This is the "Thus saith the Lord God" that Ezekiel brought at a time when the people were skeptical and cynical because they were utterly at the mercy of the pagans. There just didn't seem any use in putting their trust in God. Then Ezekiel came to preach to them, calling the heart of man to bow down to God. This is what Ezekiel was commissioned to do.

You're a believer in God. You trust in the Lord Jesus Christ, but your faith isn't strong. You have no confidence when it comes to praying about things. How can we help you? The first thing we will tell you is look to God. Then we will tell you what God has to say in His Word. Anytime the people of God are confused by hearing many voices, they need to hear one voice clear and strong—the voice of God. And through the teaching and the preaching of a godly man, there can actually be brought to the people a clear-cut call from God, a "Thus saith the Lord." It will not be the consensus of opinion found through some survey to see what everybody thinks. We look to see what the mind of God is. And this leads us out of our confusion. We look to the Lord Jesus Christ, and in Him are found "all the treasures of the Godhead in a bodily form." It will all be in Christ Jesus.

Do you realize that many persons who do not serve God, who do not even pretend to believe in Him, actually understand that Heaven is His home?

Times change, even in matters of faith. Sometimes in the history of society it is easier to believe in God than at other times. The Bible tells us that "when iniquity shall abound, the love of many shall wax cold." When it is popular not to study the Bible, and when

Daniel, "The God of Heaven Rules"

it's popular not to pray, it's because people don't feel they've lost anything. In times like that the Christian can lose his blessing by default. If you were supposed to play in a tournament and you just didn't show up, that's a default, and it's recorded that you lost. Well, this is what happens to a lot of Christians. They believe the Bible is the Word of God. They believe praying is the right thing to do. But they default. It's an easy thing for a person to accept the Lord Jesus Christ in all sincerity and turn to Him with every intention to walk faithfully with Him, but then lose out by default. He gets in with a group of people and finds out they don't go to church regularly, so he falls into the same habit. He follows the same tendency in matters of prayer, Bible study, and witnessing. When other people are doubting, it's easy to doubt. It's not easy to go contrary to the crowd, and yet this has to be done by a Christian who is going to win.

We're all interested in being on the winning side. The problem is how to determine the way that will really put you there. It's when you face this dilemma that you need someone on the scene who believes in God. It was at a time like that in Israel's history that Daniel arose. Daniel was a prisoner in a foreign country. He was among people who were all different from himself. He stood alone, but he was a man who believed in God. When all others agree that the Bible is not to be trusted, that the Scriptures are no longer valid, God raises up someone as a witness. He'll raise up a man who really believes, someone like Daniel who stands in the midst of all the unbelievers and makes no attempt to demonstrate his position by argument or comparison. He simply makes a straightforward affirmation that he will worship God and that God will take care of him. At a time when God's people have lost confidence, when they no longer are sure of things, they no longer seem to get anything out of their church services, they no longer get anything out of Bible reading, the person who affects them is the one who simply believes God. Everybody else has questions about the Bible and criticizes the Bible, ignores the Bible, uses any other kind of book in place of the Bible, and along comes a man who goes by the Bible, opens it and deals with it.

This is reflected by the interest people have today in popular hymns. It's an interesting thing that in the last few years, one of the most popular hymns has been "How Great Thou Art." The emphasis is upon the greatness of God—as it is in "Great is thy Faithfulness." People are interested in what God can do in His greatness, and it is true that with all the waywardness and all the tendency to turn away from God, there's more interest in the supernatural power of the Holy Spirit today than there has ever been. At a time when people are in trouble and are fearful and afraid, they need to know that the God of Heaven is on the Throne—that Almighty God is real and true.

Is it possible that a person can believe in God and at the same time live in distress and in trouble? Unfortunately, it is only too true! How many people there are who really do believe in God but have no blessing!

I'm writing now to people who do believe that the Bible is the Word of God, and they believe the Gospel. They know that Christ Jesus came for sinners, and they count that they are sinners. And they expect

Esther, "If I Perish, I Perish"

when they die and leave this world, that Christ Jesus will take them to Himself. And yet, these people with all those things in heart and mind can actually live their lives in fear. They believe that God holds all things in His hand, but they're afraid of tomorrow. They're afraid of what's going to happen to them, to their family, to their business, to the country, and to the world. There are people who do believe in God, and they believe in the Bible, but they are in prison. They know that God can deliver them from their sins, yet they're living in sin. Why?

We saw in the Old Testament that the people of Israel had their central city, Jerusalem, and in it was the Temple, the place where they were to worship God. And Israel's experience was supposed to be tied up with its personal relationship with God, but the people neglected the worship of God. They neglected the sacrifices of God. They neglected keeping the Sabbath Day. They were indifferent to the things of God until God finally withdrew His favor, left them to themselves, and then they were too weak to stand up. They became souls in prison. You will remember that they were taken captive by the Babylonians and carried away as prisoners into a foreign land. They were Jews, and they had the promise of God, but they had no blessing. But no matter how bad their experiences, and no matter how dark the day was for them, there was always something they could do to improve. In their darkest hour, Ezekiel the prophet blew his trumpet, and out of the night came his voice saying, "Thus saith the Lord." Later on, you will remember, when Daniel was bearing his testimony and his witness in a foreign country and in a strange city, he stood before the uneasy conscience of the King and boldly affirmed, "The God of Heaven is on the Throne!"

Now let me draw your attention to another step that could be taken. You will find it in the book of Esther, and it makes an easy reading story. Among the Jews in captivity, there was a very beautiful young woman named Esther, who was called in to be queen. Though she was one of God's people, she was given a very special place with the King and counted very fortunate. The time came, though, when the Jews were in danger of their lives, and Esther's Uncle Mordecai sent word to her that the Jews would be destroyed unless she helped them. It was a time when the Jews were in such disfavor and the things of God were so looked down upon, that even in the book of Esther the name of God is not to be found. At a time like that Mordecai sent his challenge into his niece and told her to "go into the presence of the King and talk to him about this." He told her, "Who knoweth but that thou art come to the Kingdom for such a time as this."

Esther was conscious of the risk that she would run if she went into the presence of the King without being invited, but she rose to the occasion. She told the messengers to return to Mordecai with this answer: "Go, gather together all the Jews that are present in Shushan and fast ye for me, neither eat nor drink three days, night or day: I also and my maidens will fast likewise; and so will I go in unto the king, which is not according to the law: and if I perish, I perish." These famous words are the words of desperation. Something's got to be done, and I'm the one to do it, so here goes. Whether it works out all right or not doesn't matter.

As matters turned out Esther was a means of bring ing blessing to her people. The strategy worked. But here we have our guidance for souls in prison. If it's the right thing to read the Bible, read it. If the Bible is God's Word and you want to find out His will, open it up and read it and let the chips fall where they may. "If I perish, I perish." This element of desperation needs to motivate you. Have you stopped praying? You're not really seek- ing God's face? Why don't you start—just get on your knees and pray, right in the presence of other people in your own home? You say, "They'll make fun of me." So—they'll make fun of you; they'll criticize you. Do you want to go on without the blessing? Maybe this is the very thing your whole family is waiting for. Do what needs to be done and say to yourself, "If I perish, I perish. If this is going to hurt me, let it hurt." That kind of desperation in a dark night will bring you to God.

Do you think it is ever too late to turn to God? Many Christians live their lives day in and day out without blessing. I'm speaking of people who believe in God. They're not confident. They're frightened. They don't have patience. They're irritable. They do things they don't want to do. They're having trouble in their home. They're having trouble with their neighbors. They're having trouble with themselves. They're just not being blessed.

Ezra, "Yet Now There Is Hope"

You see someone living here who's not a Christian, and across the road is a person who is a Christian, and they live just exactly alike—go to the same places, spend their money in the same way, think about the same things. The emptiness and futility of life can be understood with the man who is an unbeliever, but it's utterly unnecessary for the Christian. He's accepted Christ and made an open profession of faith, but right now he's in misery, emptiness, and in barrenness. Well, is there anything such people can do?

Once upon a time God's people were led by men like Moses and Joshua, and despite all their foolishness and their failings they followed faithfully until they came into the land. Then in the land, having the land of Canaan as their own, they became confident in themselves, in their own strength. They began to take chances with their neighbors and mingle with their neighbors like Moses warned them not to. They became careless about worshipping God in spite of Moses' warnings. They forgot God, and God let the enemy come in and overwhelm them so that they were put in bondage. But when they were in trouble, they would repent and confess their sins and turn to God, and God would bring them new blessing until they became prosperous again. Then in their prosperity they would forget God. They'd become wayward and go back over the whole thing all over again. They would be in trouble, call on God, and He would send them a Judge. This Judge would show them where they were wrong. They'd repent of their sins. They'd turn to God and would be blessed, and after a priod of blessing, they'd do the same thing over again. Finally this had happened so many times and they had become so careless that God arranged for the whole city to be destroyed. And God's people were led away as captives in great distress. But even after this judgment, God was gracious, and at the end of seventy years, He restored them to their own land. At that time their leaders were men like Ezra and Nehemiah. These men led them back into their city, and they began to rebuild the city and the Temple and to re-establish themselves in the land as the people of God. After that, in the face of new evidence that Israel had strayed again, Ezra was totally discouraged. When they wouldn't turn back to God under those circumstances, Ezra wrote, "And at the evening sacrifice I arose up from my heaviness; and having rent my garment and my mantle, I fell upon my knees, and spread out my hands unto the Lord my God, and said, O my God, I am ashamed and blush to lift up my face to thee, my God: for our iniquities are increased over our head, and our trespass is grown up unto the heavens." He deplored Israel's foolishness in these words: "And after all that is come upon us for our evil deeds, and for our great trespass, seeing that thou our God hast punished us less than our iniquities deserve, and hast given us such deliverance as this; should we again break thy commandments, and join in affinity with the people of these abominations? wouldest not thou be angry with us till thou hadst consumed us, so that there should be no remnant nor escaping? O Lord God of Israel, thou art righteous: for we remain yet escaped, as it is this day: behold, we are before thee in our trespasses: for we cannot stand before thee because of this." This is the prayer of confession of a man who says, "You have restored us and we went out and did it over again, and now there isn't anything we can do." But the story concludes, "Now when Ezra had prayed, and when he had confessed, weeping and casting himself down before the house of God, there assembled unto him out of Israel a very great congregation of men and women and children: for the people wept very sore. And Shechaniah, the son of Jehiel, one of the sons of Elam, answered and said unto Ezra, We have trespassed against our God, and have taken strange wives of the people of the land: yet now there is hope in Israel concerning this thing." "It's true we've done wrong," one of the laymen says to Ezra. "It's true we're not what we ought to be. But yet there is hope about this thing. Let us turn to God. We'll confess our sins. We'll repudiate what we've done wrong. We'll turn away from these things and we'll come to God now." At this point a layman challenged the preacher to lay hold of the grace of God. Make your confession of sin, then make a covenant with God, take a definite stand with God. Forget the things that are behind. Look forward and let it be done according to the Scriptures. Do what the Bible says.

Revival in the church is possible, but revival in the church must begin with the officers of the church, with the preacher, with the men who can lead the people. This is what has to be done. No matter how dark the night is, you can always come to the light. You can always turn to God, and in the darkest hour, the light from God will shine the brightest in your soul. No matter what your condition may be, no matter what you've been into and what you've been through, no matter where you are now, turn where you are now to God. Definitely commit yourself to Him. Forget everything in the past and once and for all settle it, that you're going to walk in the ways of God.

Do you know what to do when you're traveling across the country and you have gotten on the wrong road? Of course you do—but let me ask you another question. Was there ever a day when you were closer to the Lord than you are now? Even though you're a Christian, even though you believe in Him, you may be a person who never reads the Bible, and you may be a person that doesn't pray, and you may be a person who has never witnessed to others. Well, I can tell you right now without knowing who you are or where you live, you're not happy. You couldn't be. God wouldn't let you be. God wants you to know that you are without His presence and without His favor. Do you know what to do now that you recognize all this?

Hosea, "Let Us Return Unto the Lord"

People are in confusion today all around us. We hear voices from all directions telling us to do this and telling us to do that. You frankly don't know what's right and what's wrong. We're living in a day of confusion. In international affairs, in national affairs, in society—we don't seem to have any standards any more. Good and bad, right and wrong are confused. Spiritual experience has become uncertain.

In this state of confusion, wouldn't you agree that if anybody ought to know what to do, it would be a Christian? If there is anyone who knows where he can find help, it ought to be the man who knows God. Let us return to the Lord. That's the only place where we can get a clear word. It's God who knows, and it is God who can deliver.

But it isn't really that we don't know what to do. We don't have what it takes to do it. We don't have the inward strength. But we can't be happy that way.

Did you ever dream that some danger was threatening you, but you couldn't move? You wanted to scream, but you couldn't. Well, some people live their lives that way, and their spiritual experience is like that. It's all like a horrible dream. They need to do something, but they're weak. Now I ask you, does anybody know where strength can be found?

We know that all power is given unto the Lord. We know that He tells us to put our trust in Him. We know that "They that wait upon the Lord shall renew their strength. They shall mount up with wings as eagles. They shall run and not be weary. They shall walk and not faint." We understand that. Then what shall we do? We who know what to do in the time of weakness, when we're so weak we can't even stand up, we can turn to the Lord. Let us return to the Lord. In our weakness let us come to Him. He is strong. He can do it. Then why don't we do it? Why don't we then come to God in our perplexity and weakness? If we need help and He is our great Helper, then why don't we come?

There is one thing that keeps many of us away from turning to God. We're downright ashamed. We're ashamed of the way we have lived. We're guilty. We haven't done what we ought to have done. We have done things we ought not to have done. And the worst of it has been our neglect. We have ignored when we should have listened, and we've been careless when we should have been careful. And now we've got the feeling deep down within us—and a sickening feeling it is —that we're getting just what's coming to us. Then what shall we do?

Well, here is the solution: humble yourselves under the mighty hand of God. So you're not what you ought to be! So your record is poor! So what you have done is foolish and wrong! Then return to the Lord. "Come now, let us reason together, saith the Lord: though your sins be as scarlet, they shall be as white as snow; though they be red like crimson, they shall be as wool." We know what it means to "let the wicked forsake his way, and the unrighteous man his thoughts: let him return unto the Lord, for he will have mercy upon him; and to our God, for he will abundantly pardon." We can do like the Prodigal Son, who when he came to himself said, "How many hired servants in my father's house have bread enough and to spare, and I perish with hunger! I will arise and go to my father." This is what's needed. We simply need to say to one another, "Let us return to God. Let us come back to Him and we can find in Him all the help that we shall need."

Today we have people who are in trouble and who go everywhere looking for help. Some of them go to doctors and some to psychiatrists hoping they can find some help. When actually the trouble is that God has forsaken them. In Hosea 5:15 God says, "I will go and return to my place, till they acknowledge their offence, and seek my face: in their affliction they will seek me early." Later on we read where the prophet said, "Come, and let us return unto the Lord: for he hath torn, and he will heal us; he hath smitten, and he will bind us up. After two days will he revive us: in the third day he will raise us up, and we shall live in his sight. Then shall we know, if we follow on to know the Lord."

God is gracious. You can come to God. "Whosoever cometh unto me, I will in no wise cast out."

"Come then to the Savior and make no delay,
Here in our midst He's standing today,
tenderly saying, 'Come'."

You come to the Lord, and see how He will bless you.